C0-DUO-764

RECEIVED

JUN 06 2018

Douglass-Truth Branch Library

NO LONGER PROPERTY OF
SEATTLE PUBLIC LIBRARY

TOKYO
City Trails

Anna Claybourne

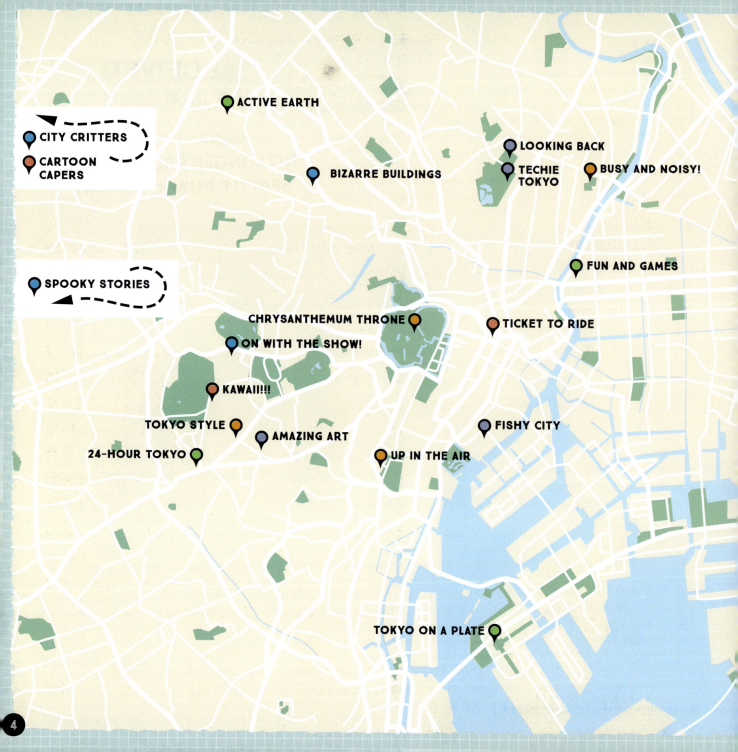

Hi... we're Amelia and Marco, and we've created 19 awesome themed trails for you to follow.

The pushpins on this map mark the starting points, and each trail is packed with insider secrets and loads of cool stuff. So whether you are a culture vulture, a sports fanatic or a history buff, this book has got something for you!

CONTENTS

PAGE NUMBER

➡ FISHY CITY 6–9
➡ ACTIVE EARTH...10–15
➡ UP IN THE AIR 16–21
➡ BIZARRE BUILDINGS..22–25
➡ KAWAII!!! 26–29
➡ TECHIE TOKYO 30–35
➡ TOKYO ON A PLATE 36–41
➡ TOKYO STYLE 42–47
➡ SPOOKY STORIES 48–53
➡ CARTOON CAPERS...54–57
➡ AMAZING ART 58–63
➡ 24-HOUR TOKYO 64–67
➡ BUSY AND NOISY! 68–71
➡ ON WITH THE SHOW! 72–75
➡ TICKET TO RIDE 76–79
➡ LOOKING BACK..80–85
➡ FUN AND GAMES 86–89
➡ CHRYSANTHEMUM THRONE 90–93
➡ CITY CRITTERS...94–99
INDEX 100–102
FURTHER READING...102

FISHY CITY

Japan is a nation of islands, surrounded by fish-filled seas. Tokyo, its capital, is a seaside city, built around Tokyo Bay – a huge natural harbor. So it's no surprise that fish are incredibly important here – in folklore, culture, art, and on the dinner table!

START → TSUKIJI FISH MARKET →

WANT SOME FISH?

TSUKIJI FISH MARKET

In Tokyo, the place to go to buy the finest fresh fish is the famous Tsukiji Market, near the harbor. Some parts of the market are only for business customers, who bid at auction for seafood, such as enormous whole tuna. But tourists and shoppers can visit the 400 stalls and cafés of the Tsukiji Outer Market. Here, they can buy fruit, vegetables, and cookware, as well as endless varieties of seafood, such as fish, shellfish, roe (fish eggs), sea urchins, jellyfish, and squid. If it comes from the sea, it's here!

TO KEEP THE MARKET AND ITS SUPER-FRESH FISH AS CLEAN AS CAN BE, THE RULES FOR VISITORS ARE STRICT. NO SMOKING, NO PETS, NO BABIES, AND NO OPEN-TOED SHOES!

PET SHOP

PAUPAU AQUA GARDEN

If you prefer your sea creatures alive, so you can keep them as pets, stop off at the PauPau Aqua Garden. They have all the tanks, fish food, and other supplies you need to keep fish at home. There's also a range of amazing animals to buy – from colorful tropical fish and shrimp to more unusual nautiluses, sea horses, and jellyfish.

SEA HORSES ARE VERY POPULAR AMONG FISH-KEEPERS – PARTLY BECAUSE PEOPLE THINK THEY LOOK LIKE DRAGONS, AND DRAGONS ARE A BIG PART OF JAPANESE FOLKLORE. IN FACT, THE JAPANESE NAME FOR "SEA HORSE" IS *TATSUNOKO* (BABY DRAGON). AWWW!

PAUPAU AQUA GARDEN

PEOPLE OFTEN THINK SUSHI MEANS RAW FISH. IN FACT, IT'S A FOOD MADE OF RICE COMBINED WITH FISH (OFTEN RAW), MEAT OR VEGETABLES, AND SOMETIMES WRAPPED IN SEAWEED. INVENTED IN JAPAN, IT HAS BECOME A HUGE HIT AROUND THE WORLD.

SUSHI SKILLS

TOKYO SUSHI ACADEMY

Sushi is prized for its beautiful appearance as well as its taste, and making it is a skilled job. Students from around the world come to study the art of sushi-making at the Tokyo Sushi Academy. A professional course lasts eight weeks, but tourists and locals can learn the basics in a speedy 90-minute sushi session.

KAITENZUSHI NEMURO HANAMARU

TOKYO SUSHI ACADEMY

SUSHI-GO-ROUND

KAITENZUSHI NEMURO HANAMARU

At lunchtime, thousands of busy workers need to grab a quick bite to eat. To make serving as quick and easy as possible, the Japanese invented *kaitenzushi* (conveyor-belt sushi). A long conveyor belt winds around the room past all the tables, carrying plates of food. All you need to do is pick your favorites, then pay when you've finished eating! This *kaitenzushi* restaurant in downtown Tokyo is one of the city's most popular conveyor-belt eateries.

FEED THE FISH
KOISHIKAWA KŌRAKUEN GARDENS

Step into this beautiful garden, and you're in another world – a haven of peace and nature in the middle of the bustling city. The park was created in the 1600s, and it has a pond filled with gleaming silver and orange koi carp. You can buy some special food from the garden shop, then feed the fish from the ancient bridges or stepping stones.

search: KOI CARP

📍 FEARLESS FISH

In Japan, the koi carp is seen as a symbol of strength, persistence, and courage. There is a long tradition of keeping them in ponds in parks and gardens. Colorful koi-shaped streamers are flown to celebrate Children's Day in May.

FISH CAKE!
NEZU NO TAIYAKI

Vegetarian? No problem! You can enjoy a delicious fish-shaped snack at Nezu No Taiyaki. *Taiyaki* (baked sea bream) is actually a pancake made in the shape of a sea bream fish. It's filled with *anko*, a sweet, jam-like bean paste. Nezu No Taiyaki is one of the oldest *taiyaki* stalls in the city – it's been serving up the fish-shaped snacks for over 50 years.

WHY SHAPE A PANCAKE LIKE A SEA BREAM? SOME SAY IT'S BECAUSE REAL SEA BREAM USED TO BE SO EXPENSIVE, CHEFS INVENTED THE PANCAKE VERSION AS A CHEAP ALTERNATIVE TREAT. OR IT COULD BE BECAUSE THE SEA BREAM'S NAME, *TAI*, ALSO MEANS "HAPPY."

"It doesn't taste like fish."

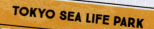

ALL OVER THE CITY

FUGU

ALL OVER THE CITY

Fugu is the Japanese word for "pufferfish," a fish that contains lethal poison – but is still eaten as a delicacy! Specialist fugu chefs learn how to remove the majority of the dangerous parts, leaving just enough poison in the fish to give the eater a tingly sensation in their mouth. Fugu restaurants often have a lantern outside, made from the skin of a pufferfish.

OCEAN WORLD

TOKYO SEA LIFE PARK

Looking across Tokyo Bay, a space-age glass dome seems to rise out of the water. This is the Tokyo Sea Life Park, Tokyo's biggest aquarium. Here, you can see fish from around the world in a range of ocean habitats, from tropical coral reefs to polar seas. It's famous for its enormous ring-shaped tuna tank, where shoals of bluefin tuna zoom around viewers. Fed up of fish? The park also has one of the world's largest penguin exhibits!

THE SEA PARADISE AQUARIUM IN YOKOHAMA HAS A GIGANTIC TANK FILLED WITH OVER 50,000 SARDINES! THEY SWIM AROUND IN A HUGE SHOAL WITH LIGHTS AND MUSIC, IN A DISPLAY KNOWN AS THE "SUPER SARDINE ILLUSION."

ACTIVE EARTH

All over Japan, there's a high risk of earthquakes, tsunamis, and volcanic eruptions. That's because four of the giant tectonic plates that make up the Earth's crust meet here, and one of the boundaries runs very close to Tokyo. People have to know what to do if disaster strikes – but the active Earth also makes for some amazing sights and experiences.

SHAKE IT UP

EARTHQUAKE HALL

A trip to the Earthquake Hall is probably a good place to start! Part museum and part safety center, visitors can hold on tight and experience what some of Tokyo's biggest and deadliest quakes felt like in its earthquake simulator. They can also pick up survival tips, such as crawling under a sturdy table and putting a cushion on your head. Could come in handy!

search: CATFISH AND QUAKES

 EARTH-SHAKER

According to Japanese folklore, earthquakes are caused by Namazu, a giant catfish that lives in the mud at the bottom of Tokyo Bay, or under the islands of Japan. A god named Kashima keeps the catfish still under a heavy stone most of the time, but sometimes Namazu manages to wriggle, setting off a quake.

QUAKE ALERT

We now know quakes are really caused by the movement of tectonic plates – but catfish do seem to be able to predict earthquakes, thrashing and wriggling about just before they happen. This could be where the story came from.

QUAKE MEMORIES

KANTŌ EARTHQUAKE MEMORIAL MUSEUM

One of the worst earthquake disasters in world history struck Tokyo just before midday on September 1, 1923. Called the Great Kantō Earthquake, it destroyed most of the city, and over 140,000 people died. This museum tells the story of what happened, and acts as a memorial to many of the dead, whose ashes are stored here. Visitors can also see objects that were damaged in the quake and by the huge fires that spread through the city in its aftermath.

 START

EARTHQUAKE HALL

KANTŌ EARTHQUAKE MEMORIAL MUSEUM

QUAKE-PROOF TOWER

YOKOHAMA LANDMARK TOWER

Down by the harbor in Yokohama, this imposing, 70-story tower is one of many skyscrapers built to withstand earthquakes. Its flexible structure is similar to that of a traditional Japanese pagoda, and helps it move and sway in an earthquake instead of collapsing. Visitors head to the 69th floor, where the observation deck offers an amazing view of the whole Tokyo area — and, on a clear day, the famous volcano, Mount Fuji.

11:58 A.M.
SEPTEMBER 1, 1923
THE TIME THE GREAT KANTŌ EARTHQUAKE BEGAN

40 FT. (15 M)
HEIGHT OF THE TSUNAMIS CAUSED BY THE QUAKE

142,800 ESTIMATED NUMBER OF DEAD

MUCH OF MODERN TOKYO LOOKS THE WAY IT DOES BECAUSE IT HAD TO BE REBUILT AFTER THE 1923 EARTHQUAKE. PLANNERS INCLUDED LOTS OF PARKS AND OPEN SPACES TO GIVE PEOPLE PLACES TO RUN TO IF A QUAKE STRUCK.

ABOUT TO BLOW?

Fuji is an active volcano, and although it doesn't erupt often, it could go off at some point soon! Scientific studies show enough pressure is building up inside to power an almighty blast.

JAPAN'S SNOW CONE

MOUNT FUJI

Japan's highest mountain and most famous volcano is just a day trip away from Tokyo. It is renowned for its beautifully perfect cone shape, capped with gleaming white snow in winter. It's been a sacred site since ancient times, and is a national symbol of Japan.

THE JAPANESE CALL MOUNT FUJI "FUJISAN," MEANING "FUJI MOUNTAIN." OTHER NAMES INCLUDE "FUJIYAMA" AND "HUZI."

1707
LAST ERUPTION

HEIGHT
12,389 FT.
(3,776 M)

300,000
AVERAGE NUMBER OF PEOPLE WHO CLIMB TO THE TOP EACH YEAR

6 HOURS
THE TIME IT TAKES TO CLIMB MOUNT FUJI (ON A GOOD DAY)

FOREST OF DOOM

If you're easily spooked, stay away from Aokigahara Forest, at the bottom of Mount Fuji, one of the world's creepiest locations. It's said to be haunted by countless *yurei*, or spirits of the dead. Beneath the forest, there's a cave filled with ice all year round. The trees are so thick that the forest is almost silent inside, and there's hardly any wildlife. It's so easy to get lost there that people lay trails of plastic tape to help them find their way out!

UP TO THE TOP!

Hundreds of thousands of visitors attempt to climb Mount Fuji every year. It may seem like a simple stroll up a smooth hillside – but it's not as easy as it looks! Fuji is steep, and dangers include avalanches, strong winds, and icy cold weather. To stay safe, it's important to stick to the official climbing season in the summer.

CABLE CAR RIDE

FOR A SLIGHTLY EASIER OPTION, TOURISTS CAN TAKE A CABLE CAR UP NEARBY MOUNT TENJO, ON THE KACHI KACHI YAMA ROPEWAY. AT THE TOP IS A VIEWING PLATFORM WITH AN AWESOME VIEW OF MOUNT FUJI (ON A CLEAR DAY!) AND LAKE KAWAGUCHI BELOW.

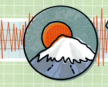

BOILING VALLEY

ŌWAKUDANI

Close to Mount Fuji is Hakone, a popular vacation area, filled with lakes, mountains, and volcanic hot springs. Via a cable car, tourists can visit Ōwakudani, meaning "great boiling valley." It's a strange, alien-looking crater left behind after a gigantic volcanic eruption 3,000 years ago. The valley has hot springs, hot rivers, and sulfurous-smelling steam vents.

NO VISIT TO ŌWAKUDANI IS COMPLETE WITHOUT EATING *KURO-TAMAGO*, OR EGGS BOILED IN THE SULFUR-RICH HOT SPRINGS, WHICH GIVES THEM A BLACK SHELL. THEY ARE SAID TO BE SO HEALTHY THAT EATING ONE ADDS SEVEN YEARS TO YOUR LIFE!

OUTDOOR SPA

YUNESSUN ONSEN

The Hakone area has many *onsen* (hot spring spas) where the volcanic spring water is the perfect temperature for bathing in. The mineral-filled spring water is said to have health benefits, such as curing headaches or eczema. At Yunessun Onsen, there are also green tea, coffee, wine, sake (Japanese rice wine), and chocolate spa baths, as well as water slides!

HOT SPRINGS FORM IN VOLCANIC AREAS, WHERE THERE ARE POCKETS OF HOT MAGMA (MOLTEN ROCK) NOT FAR BENEATH THE EARTH'S SURFACE. THE MAGMA HEATS UP UNDERGROUND WATER, WHICH THEN FLOWS TO THE SURFACE OR CAN BE PUMPED OUT.

IN JAPAN'S FAMOUS *GODZILLA* FILMS,
THE MONSTER GODZILLA WAS IMPRISONED
IN MOUNT MIHARA'S CRATER.

VOLCANO ISLAND

IZU ŌSHIMA

Izu Ōshima is an island south
of Tokyo Bay. Though it's over
60 miles (100 km) away, it's
actually part of the city of
Tokyo. Covered in colorful
camellia flowers, the whole
island is dominated by Mount
Mihara (an active volcano),
and has its own hot spring spa
as well as a volcano museum.

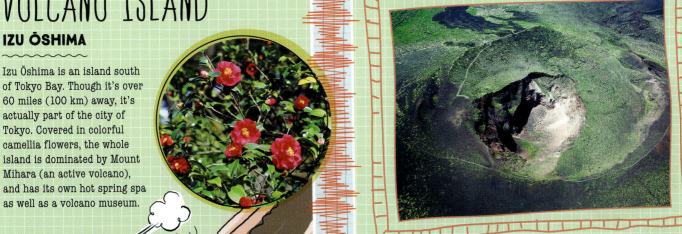

INTO THE ABYSS

MOUNT MIHARA CRATER

There's no need to trek to the top of
Mount Mihara – there's a road all the
way up so you can go by bus!
At the summit, there's a huge, deep,
scary volcanic crater, which sometimes
bubbles with hot lava.

UP IN THE AIR

Like any decent mega-city, Tokyo has fantastic skyscrapers, including some of the world's biggest and most spectacular. Visitors can take in the view from observation decks at the top of the city's many tall towers, or take to the skies with real and virtual flying machines.

"How will I find my friend?"

LOUISE BOURGEOIS'S SPIDER SCULPTURE OUTSIDE MORI TOWER IS A FAVORITE MEETING PLACE.

START

TOKYO TOWER

ROPPONGI HILLS

THE TOWER IS WHITE AND INTERNATIONAL ORANGE – A COLOR USED TO HELP AIRCRAFT STEER CLEAR OF TALL STRUCTURES.

TOWERING TRIANGLE

TOKYO TOWER

It may not be the tallest, or the newest – but you certainly can't miss it! Tokyo Tower was completed in 1958 to broadcast color television across the city, and it became a symbol of Japan's post-war success. It's based on France's famous Eiffel Tower, with the same triangular shape. However, it's taller, lighter, and a lot more colorful. You can take the elevator or the stairs to two observation decks.

SPACE IS IN SHORT SUPPLY IN TOKYO, SO UNLIKE THE EIFFEL TOWER, TOKYO TOWER HAS A FOUR-STORY BUILDING BENEATH IT, KNOWN AS "FOOT TOWN." IT CONTAINS MUSEUMS, SHOPS, CAFÉS, AND A MANGA-THEMED GAME CENTER.

MINI-CITY

ROPPONGI HILLS

The upmarket district of Roppongi is home to construction tycoon Minoru Mori's micro-city, Roppongi Hills. It's designed so people can live, work, shop, relax, and exercise all in one tiny area. It has apartments, a park, a movie theater, and an arena, as well as a whopping skyscraper, the Mori Tower. Inside it are offices, an art gallery, nightclubs, shops, and restaurants – it even has an observation deck.

LEARNING COCOON
MODE GAKUEN COCOON TOWER

This stunning skyscraper is home to three colleges: one of fashion, one of technology and design, and one of medicine. The unique building was designed with a cocoon shape to represent the way that it nurtures and develops its students.

COMPLETED IN 1990, TOKYO METROPOLITAN GOVERNMENT BUILDING WAS DESIGNED TO LOOK LIKE A COMPUTER CHIP BY ARCHITECT KENZŌ TANGE!

FREE VIEWS
TOKYO METROPOLITAN GOVERNMENT BUILDING

Observation decks often charge a fee, but this building has two totally free viewing platforms, one in each tower. From here you can not only see some of Tokyo's tallest skyscrapers, but also – on a clear day – get a view of faraway Mount Fuji.

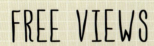

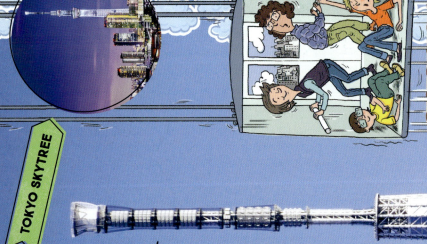

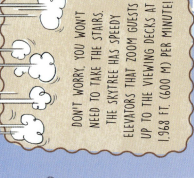

TOKYO SKYTREE

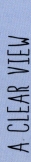

DON'T WORRY. YOU WON'T NEED TO TAKE THE STAIRS. THE SKYTREE HAS SPEEDY ELEVATORS THAT ZOOM GUESTS UP TO THE VIEWING DECKS AT 1,968 FT. (600 M) PER MINUTE!

WHY "SKYTREE"? THE NAME WAS CHOSEN FROM A LIST OF SIX NAMES SUGGESTED BY MEMBERS OF THE PUBLIC IN A NATIONWIDE SURVEY.

WORLD'S TALLEST TREE

TOKYO SKYTREE

So you've seen some soaring skyscrapers... but wait... there's more! One of Tokyo's structures really does tower above the rest. It's called Tokyo Skytree, and it opened in 2012. At a mind-boggling 2,080 ft. (634 m) high, it's not only Japan's highest tower, but also the second-tallest structure in the world (after Dubai's Burj Khalifa). Skytree is mainly a broadcasting tower, sending out TV and radio signals. But it's also open to the public, with shops, cafés, and two hair-raisingly high viewing decks.

A CLEAR VIEW

Don't look down! Or actually, do... because Skytree has several see-through features to give visitors the most breathtaking views possible. The lower observation deck, Tembo Deck, has a glass floor where you can look straight down to the ground 1,148 ft. (350 m) below. Higher up, there's the glass Tembo Galleria that winds around the outside of the tower, 1,476 ft. (450 m) up!

LIGHTING UP

Many of Tokyo's landmarks light up at night, and when Skytree was built, 1,995 LED lighting units were installed to make sure it played its part. Two main colors illuminate it at night:

IKI BLUE

This color represents simplicity, stylishness, and originality, and the Sumida River that Skytree sits next to.

MIYABI PURPLE

This color represents elegance, refinement, and courage.

SKYTREE TOWN

Skytree is part of a bigger development, Skytree Town, with even more things for tourists to see and do. At ground level, all around the tower, there are hundreds of shops and places to eat – there's even an aquarium!

FIREWORKS SHOW

Each July, the incredible Sumidagawa Fireworks Festival takes place in Asakusa district, across the Sumida River from Skytree. On that night, a lottery is held for tickets to Skytree's observation decks for the best view of the show.

HOW HIGH?

Tokyo Skytree 2,080 ft. (634 m)

Tokyo Tower 1,092 ft. (333 m)

Tokyo Metropolitan Government Building 799 ft. (243 m)

Mori Tower 781 ft. (238 m)

Mode Gakuen Cocoon Tower 668 ft. (204 m)

Daikanransha Ferris Wheel 377 ft. (115 m)

TAKE-OFF!

URAYASU HELIPORT

If you want to catch your own sightseeing helicopter flight around the city, all you need to do is head across Tokyo Bay to the handy heliport at Urayasu. This is where Tokyo's many helicopter tours take off. The choppers fly at around 2,300 ft. (700 m) – slightly higher than the top of Tokyo Skytree, so you'll get an amazing view.

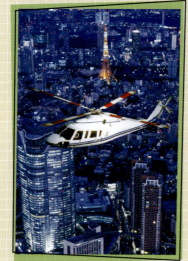

WHEELY HIGH!

DAIKANRANSHA

Staying a little closer to the ground, a ride on Daikanransha, a giant Ferris wheel in Odaiba, is a great way to see the harbor area. The wheel is 328 ft. (100 m) in diameter, but as it's raised off the ground, it reaches a height of 377 ft. (115 m) at the top. It's also covered in lights that create illuminated patterns and animations at night.

DAIKANRANSHA

"Oh no,... I've dropped my phone!"

search: FLYING MACHINES

📍 **BIG BLIMP**
In 2010, an enormous airship made tours over Tokyo for just a few months. The blimp rides are no longer running, but airships are said to be one of the transportation modes of the future – so they could be back!

📍 **JET PACK JOURNEY**
In 2013, Swiss daredevil Yves Rossy flew around Mount Fuji in a jet pack wingsuit – just a pair of wings strapped to his back, powered by a rocket engine.

HANEDA AIRPORT OBSERVATION DECK

PLANE-SPOTTER'S PARADISE

HANEDA AIRPORT OBSERVATION DECK

If you like watching planes taking off and landing, you'll be in heaven at Haneda Airport. This isn't Tokyo's main international airport (that's Narita, out east of the city). Haneda is a smaller airport in Tokyo Bay, but has one of the world's biggest observation decks. Besides watching planes and checking out lots of aircraft diagrams and models, you can have a go in a flight simulation machine and practice flying and landing.

"Look, Dad, the pilot's waving at us!"

KITE CRAZINESS

SHOWA-MACHI GIANT KITE FESTIVAL

The Japanese have a history of kite-flying going back hundreds of years. Kite festivals are still held all over Japan, especially in spring, to fly *odako* (humongous kites made of bamboo and paper). The Showa-Machi Kite Festival takes place every May, on the banks of the Edo River in Saitama, just north of the city. The huge rectangular kites are as big as 33 ft. (11 m) by 40 ft. (15 m), and it can take up to 100 people pulling the rope to get them into the air.

SHOWA-MACHI GIANT KITE FESTIVAL

1,776 SQ. FT. SIZE OF BIGGEST **ODAKO KITES** THAT'S THE AREA OF A SPACIOUS APARTMENT!

AD 600 THE CENTURY WHEN KITE FLYING TOOK OFF IN JAPAN

1.1 TONS THE WEIGHT OF A LARGE ODAKO KITE

BIZARRE BUILDINGS

As one of the world's biggest and most modern cities, Tokyo is packed with every kind of crazy construction you can imagine... and quite a few you can't. Take this trail to spot some of the most brain-boggling buildings you've ever seen, from a robot-shaped school to a golden poop!

MANY CITIES HAVE STRICT RULES ABOUT WHAT BUILDINGS CAN LOOK LIKE OR BE MADE OF. IN TOKYO, ALTHOUGH BUILDINGS MUST BE EARTHQUAKE PROOF, ARCHITECTS ARE PRETTY FREE TO DESIGN WHAT THEY LIKE. THE MIX OF BUILDINGS IS UNIQUE AND STRIKING, AND ADDS TO TOKYO'S VIBRANT ATMOSPHERE.

START

ST. MARY'S CATHEDRAL

IIDABASHI SUBWAY STATION

IT'S ALIVE!
IIDABASHI SUBWAY STATION

If you have to catch a train at this subway station, you'll see a bit of Japanese bio-architecture: buildings inspired by the natural world. Outside one entrance, a huge metal flower with steel petal and leaf shapes sprouts around an air vent. Inside, a web of bright green pipes leads you deeper underground, making the tunnels and passageways feel like caves overgrown with hi-tech vines.

SHINING WINGS
ST. MARY'S CATHEDRAL

This famous cathedral was once a much more traditional wooden building, until it was flattened during air raids in World War II. After the war, top Japanese architect Kenzō Tange decided to create something super-modern instead. Its stainless-steel-covered walls, surrounding a basic cross shape, gleam in the sunlight like silvery wings.

"Are you my mommy?"

BUILDING BLOCKS

NAKAGIN CAPSULE TOWER

This cube-covered tower was created according to the concept that buildings might be able to grow and change. Its cubes, or capsules, are bolted onto a concrete tower core. Each capsule can be used as a mini-apartment or office. They can be easily taken off, replaced, and rearranged. The tower is sadly a bit old and dilapidated these days, but people still live and work in it.

ASAHI BEER
HEADQUARTERS

NAKAGIN CAPSULE
TOWER

THE POOP BUILDING

ASAHI BEER HEADQUARTERS

Head east across the Sumida River for a glimpse of the famous "golden poop" (or *kin no unko* in Japanese). That's what locals call the strange, gold-painted squiggle on top of the Asahi Beer Hall. Perhaps not what Asahi, one of Japan's top beverage companies, had in mind when they created their HQ! The tall tower is meant to look like a glass of beer with foam on top, while the "poop" is meant to be a golden flame on top of a beer glass. Obviously!

THE "POOP" IS THE CREATION OF FAMOUS FRENCH DESIGNER PHILIPPE STARCK. IT'S CONSTRUCTED FROM STEEL, WEIGHS 397 TONS, AND IS COMPLETELY HOLLOW.

search: KŌBAN

CALL THE POLICE!

Kōban are Japanese police boxes. They are like local mini-police stations dotted around the city, where locals can report a crime or ask the police for help. They are often built in unusual styles, and some are the work of famous architects. Look for:

The bizarre sci-fi-style kōban at Ueno Park.

Udagawa kōban in Shibuya district, which looks like an owl, an ax, or a bird's beak.

The pointy-roofed kōban in Ginza shopping district, which looks like a fairy-tale cottage.

THE SPACESHIP HAS LANDED!

REIYUKAI SHAKADEN TEMPLE

Right in the middle of bustling Minato in central Tokyo, nestled among apartment blocks and offices, is a vast, black, pyramid-shaped spaceship. It landed there in 1975 – no, wait! – it was built in 1975, and it's actually a temple. This amazing building is the HQ of a modern Japanese religion, Reiyukai. With its dark granite cladding and cavernous doorway, it looks scary – but is actually a friendly social center where people can meet up and take classes. It's open to everyone.

REIYUKAI SHAKADEN TEMPLE

AOYAMA TECHNICAL COLLEGE

"I'll teach you!"

THE ROBOT RISES

AOYAMA TECHNICAL COLLEGE

When you first spot this school of technical design on a quiet residential street in Shibuya, it can give you a bit of a scare! It appears to have a huge, hi-tech robot with insect-like antennae rising out of it, about to attack the old-fashioned houses next door. Some people hate it, but you can't deny it looks pretty technical!

THE ICEBERG

AUDI FORUM

This jagged tower is the Tokyo office of German car company Audi. It's nicknamed the "Iceberg" thanks to its zigzag shape, made of gleaming glass, which spikes up into the sky. It looks especially stunning at night, when it's lit up in shimmering white and blue. According to its designers, in addition to icebergs, they found inspiration from a plastic bottle after it's gone through a recycling shredder!

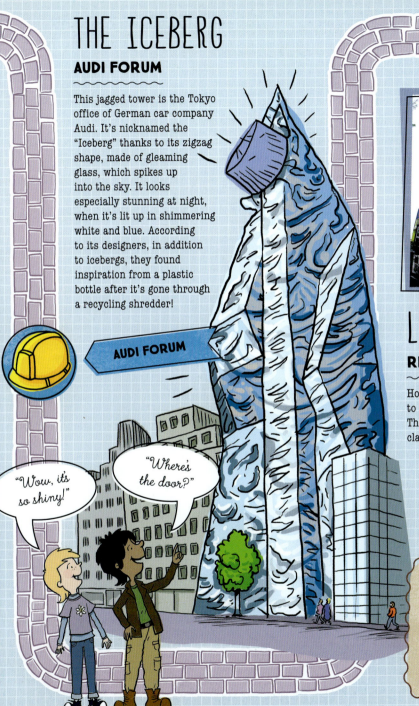

AUDI FORUM

"Wow, it's so shiny!"

"Where's the door?"

REVERSIBLE DESTINY LOFTS

LIVE FOREVER!

REVERSIBLE DESTINY LOFTS

How would you like to live in an apartment that's designed to change your life – or perhaps even help you live longer? That's what this colorful apartment block in western Tokyo claims to do. The homes are as odd-looking on the inside as on the outside, and were created to make residents question life and do things differently. They have awkward spaces, strange echo effects, bumpy floors, round rooms, and many other unexpected features. The idea is to challenge and exercise your mind, which makes you live longer – or "reverse your destiny"!

THE REVERSIBLE DESTINY LOFTS WERE DESIGNED BY HUSBAND-AND-WIFE ARCHITECTURAL TEAM MADELINE GINS AND SHUSAKU ARAKAWA. THEY NAMED THEIR PHILOSOPHY "ARCHITECTURE AGAINST DEATH" AND DECLARED, "WE HAVE DECIDED NOT TO DIE." SADLY, THEY BOTH DIED IN THEIR 70S – BUT LIVED TO SEE THEIR LOFTS COMPLETED IN 2005.

KAWAII!!!

Kawaii is a Japanese word that means cute... or adorable, lovable, dinky, or pretty. Kawaii is a central part of Japanese culture and design, and it's not just for children. Kawaii designs are found everywhere!

START

TAKESHITA STREET, HARAJUKU

CUTE CENTRAL

TAKESHITA STREET

The cuteness trail kicks off in Harajuku, a fashionable shopping district popular with teenagers and tourists. It's the center of all things *kawaii*! The most famous street of all is Takeshita, where you can buy toys, stationery, candy, make-up, clothes, bags, lunch boxes, and anything else you can think of – all with cute characters, animals, flowers, or slogans.

TOO SWEET TO EAT!

POMPOMPURIN CAFÉ

Pompompurin is a super-cute character who's been around since 1996. He's a cartoon golden retriever dog with a brown beret. Besides buying items decorated with their favorite dog, fans can visit the Pompompurin Café, in a mall on Takeshita Street called the Cute Cube! Not only is the café bright yellow and covered in Pompompurin designs, it also serves Pompompurin-shaped food.

POMPOMPURIN CAFÉ

SANRIOWORLD GINZA

BUY KAWAII

SANRIOWORLD GINZA

Sanrio designs and sells famous lovable characters such as Pompompurin and Hello Kitty. Fans will be in cuteness heaven at the huge SanrioWorld store in Ginza. It's jammed to the rafters with cards, bags, boxes, jewelry, cosmetics, and clothes decorated with Sanrio's many characters. There's even a salon where you can have your favorite characters painted onto your nails.

COLOR CRAZY

KAWAII MONSTER CAFÉ

This café in Harajuku takes cuteness to a whole new level. Its owners say Harajuku district is like a monster that devours every style and culture, and becomes ever more colorful, cute, and crazy. The café has several themed areas, including a cake-shaped merry-go-round, a bar with huge glowing jellyfish, and a mushroom disco. The waiters are dressed in bright *kawaii* costumes, and even the food – which includes rainbow pasta and candy salad – is multicolored.

YOU DON'T HAVE TO EAT AT THE KAWAII MONSTER CAFÉ. IF YOU PREFER, YOU CAN JUST PAY A SMALL ENTRANCE FEE TO WANDER AROUND AND HAVE A LOOK. IT'S LIKE A CRAZY KAWAII MUSEUM!

search: HELLO KITTY

CUTE CAT TAKEOVER

- Hello Kitty is Sanrio's most successful and popular character. She's familiar all around the world, not just in Japan.

- Kitty is a cat-like character who usually wears red or pink. She's famous for her very simple design, and for having no mouth.

- Hello Kitty was created in 1974. She's over 40 years old!

MEET A MOOMIN!

MOOMIN HOUSE

The Japanese aren't just obsessed with their own cute creations – they also love cute characters from other countries. They are big fans of Finnish style. The two countries are very different, but both have a love of simple, nature-inspired design. This café and shop at Tokyo Skytree (see page 18) celebrates the famous Finnish storybook characters, the Moomins. And as you can see, the Moomins really do have a very *kawaii* look about them!

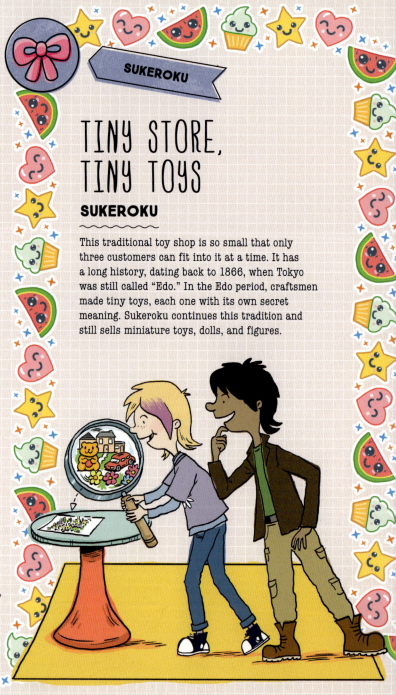

SUKEROKU

TINY STORE, TINY TOYS

SUKEROKU

This traditional toy shop is so small that only three customers can fit into it at a time. It has a long history, dating back to 1866, when Tokyo was still called "Edo." In the Edo period, craftsmen made tiny toys, each one with its own secret meaning. Sukeroku continues this tradition and still sells miniature toys, dolls, and figures.

TEENY TREES

THE OMIYA BONSAI ART MUSEUM

Cute cats, cute toys, and cute Moomins – but can trees be cute? In Japan, they can! The *kawaii* trend took off in the 20th century, but bonsai – the art of training trees to stay small – is an ancient tradition. It takes years of dedication and skill to prune, shape, and nurture a tree so it fully matures but stays the size of a potted plant. A tiny-yet-old bonsai tree is a magical sight. Japan has many bonsai gardens and nurseries where you can see them, including the Omiya Bonsai Art Museum.

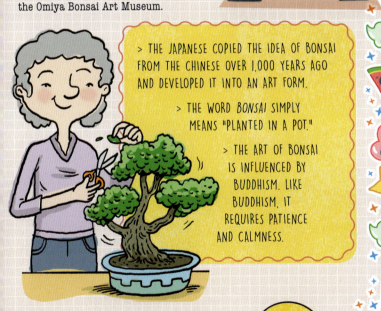

> THE JAPANESE COPIED THE IDEA OF BONSAI FROM THE CHINESE OVER 1,000 YEARS AGO AND DEVELOPED IT INTO AN ART FORM.

> THE WORD *BONSAI* SIMPLY MEANS "PLANTED IN A POT."

> THE ART OF BONSAI IS INFLUENCED BY BUDDHISM. LIKE BUDDHISM, IT REQUIRES PATIENCE AND CALMNESS.

OMIYA BONSAI ART MUSEUM

SLEEP IN A POD!

ALL OVER THE CITY

Capsule, or pod, hotels are a space-saving (and money-saving) way to spend the night somewhere safe and warm, and are common in Tokyo. Each guest climbs into a pod only slightly bigger than they are, with just enough room for a mattress, a lamp, and sometimes a tiny TV. Hope you're not claustrophobic!

WHY DO THE JAPANESE LOVE SMALL THINGS SO MUCH? ONE REASON MAY BE THAT THERE'S SO LITTLE LIVING SPACE THERE. JAPAN'S LANDSCAPE IS MOUNTAINOUS AND VOLCANIC, WITH VERY LITTLE FLAT LAND FOR BUILDING ON. SO THE JAPANESE APPRECIATE SMALL HOMES, HOTELS, STORES, AND BARS – AND TINY THINGS TO GO IN THEM!

TECHIE TOKYO

Though Japan celebrates simplicity, nature, and tradition, it also does the total opposite. It leads the world in hi-tech inventions, electronics, and robotics. Take this trail to encounter androids, inventions, and gadgets galore – including the world's most advanced toilets!

START

NATIONAL MUSEUM OF NATURE AND SCIENCE

AKIHABARA

A HISTORY OF INVENTION

NATIONAL MUSEUM OF NATURE AND SCIENCE

The Japanese have always been great inventors, and you can see a range of cool technology from past to present at this grand old Tokyo museum. It includes the work of compulsive inventor Tanaka Hisashige, who lived in the 1800s and built clocks, watches, pumps, and steam engines, as well as clockworks and automated dolls and human figures. They were an early version of the robots Japan is now famous for.

A DRESS WOVEN IN GLOWING SILK, SHOWN AT THE "HIKARI" EXHIBITION

TECHNO TOWN

AKIHABARA

All computer geeks visiting Tokyo make Akihabara number one on their must-see list. This electronics shopping district is the place to buy all kinds of gadgets, computers, video games, cameras, and techno bits and pieces for building your own machines from scratch.

MOST OF THE TECHNOLOGY FOR SALE IN AKIHABARA IS UP-TO-THE MINUTE, BUT AT THE STRANGELY NAMED SUPER POTATO STORE, YOU CAN STEP BACK IN TIME TO PLAY (AND ALSO BUY) AN AMAZING ARRAY OF RETRO VIDEO GAMES.

BLESS MY TECH!

KANDA MYOJIN SHRINE

Not far from Akihabara is a shrine, or holy place, belonging to the ancient Shintō religion, which plays a very important part in Japanese life. People visit shrines to ask for blessings and good luck – and this shrine specializes in helping computer lovers and nerds! It's the place to go to ask for your electronic devices and tech to be blessed and protected from harm.

THE KANDA SHRINE EVEN SELLS SPECIAL CHARMS, DESIGNED TO LOOK LIKE COMPUTER CHIPS.

search: JAPANESE INVENTIONS

FLOPPY DISK
Famous eccentric inventor Yoshiro Nakamatsu helped invent this early storage device for personal computers.

POCKET CALCULATOR
Mini-electronic calculators were launched by Japanese companies in 1970.

CD PLAYER
Some of the first CD music players were released by Sony in 1982.

PLAYSTATION
Invented by Tokyo electronics engineer Ken Kutaragi in the early 1990s.

TOKYO SCIENCE MUSEUM

SCIENCE DAY OUT

TOKYO SCIENCE MUSEUM

Head a little way west to Kitanomaru Park to visit another awesome attraction, Tokyo's Science Museum, with its wacky, cog-shaped building. Visitors can explore computers, electricity, cars, and robots, as well as the technology of the future, through interactive hands-on exhibits.

ROBOT WORLD

HI-TECH TOKYO

Think of the ultimate sci-fi future tech, and you'll probably think of human-shaped robots that will help with household jobs, or even become our friends. In Tokyo, you can see some of the latest developments in robot technology – as well as a whole host of robot-themed art and design.

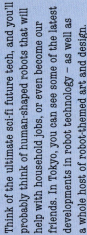

OTONAROID (ADULT) ROBOT

NATIONAL MUSEUM OF NATURE AND SCIENCE

TOO REAL!

Japan's robot brainiacs have developed realistic androids – robots designed to look and act just like humans. Two of the best known are Otonoroid (left) and Kodomoroid (above). Feeling a bit spooked? It turns out that robots that look only slightly human, like Asimo, seem cute – while those that closely resemble humans freak us out!

GIANT GUNDAM

If a 59 ft. (18 m) tall space-age robot catches your eye on the skyline as you roam downtown Tokyo, don't panic! It's not coming to take over the city. This is a model Gundam robot, a giant cartoon robot featured in a popular sci-fi animation series. Gundam robots are a type of *mecha* – armored robots that can be controlled by a human sitting somewhere inside them. Could this idea come true one day? If it does, they will probably be made in Japan!

CUTE ASIMO

The human body is pretty complicated, so it's hard to design robots that move in the same way and do the same things, such as running, dancing, or walking up and down stairs.

But several Tokyo companies have tried. The most famous robot, Asimo, was developed by car company Honda. It was first released in the year 2000.

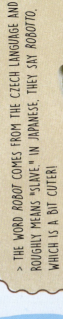

> THE WORD *ROBOT* COMES FROM THE CZECH LANGUAGE AND ROUGHLY MEANS "SLAVE." IN JAPANESE, THEY SAY *ROBOTTO*, WHICH IS A BIT CUTER!

> SONY'S LOVABLE ROBOT DOG, AIBO, WAS A HUGE HIT WHEN IT WAS LAUNCHED FOR SALE TO THE PUBLIC IN 1999.

> IN 2013, TOKYO UNIVERSITY SENT A SMALL ROBOT NAMED KIROBO TO THE INTERNATIONAL SPACE STATION, ALONGSIDE JAPANESE ASTRONAUT KOICHI WAKATA.

KAWAII ROBOT!

Of course, the *kawaii* trend (see pages 26–29) extends to robots, too. The manga character Doraemon is a time-traveling robot cat who comes from the future to help a present-day boy, Nobita. Like other cute designs, he pops up on backpacks, pencil cases, plates, and a gazillion other things.

ROBOT PARK

In some cultures, robots are seen as scary sci-fi creations that could take over the world. In Japan, though, they have a much better image, and are thought of as cute, sweet, and helpful. Tokyo's Sakurazaka Park, or Robot Park, is filled with fun robot figures and robot-shaped toys for children to play on.

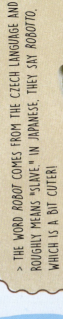

立ち止まらずに
お進み下さい

TECHNO TOILETS

TOTO TOILET SHOWROOM

Never been to a toilet showroom? Step this way! In Japan, even toilets haven't escaped the hi-tech treatment. Bathroom company Toto has a range of the most futuristic toilets to choose from. They come with an array of buttons and electronic options, and some even have their own remote control. Techno toilet functions include heating the seat, spraying warm water at your rear end, blow-drying, automatic lid-closing and flushing, and playing music or a flowing river noise to cover up the sounds of toilet use.

CAUGHT ON CAMERA

FUJIFILM SQUARE

Fujifilm is a famous Japanese company that makes photographic film for cameras – as well as photographic paper, cameras, printers, scanners, photocopiers, film for movies and X-rays, and many more amazing optical inventions. The company has its own showroom and museum at Fujifilm Square, where you can see how photography began and how it's changed over time.

TOKYO TOILET TALK

WASHLET®

A TOTO MODEL THAT WASHES THE USER'S REAR END WITH A JET OF WATER.

OTEARAI

LIKE "RESTROOM," THIS IS A POLITE WAY TO SAY "BATHROOM."

TOIRE

A MORE EVERYDAY WORD FOR THE BATHROOM.

HANDS-ON FUN

SONY EXPLORASCIENCE

Not to be outdone, world-famous tech company Sony also has its own museum nearby. It explores how its products use science, light, and sound – and it has a room full of geeky interactive gadgets.

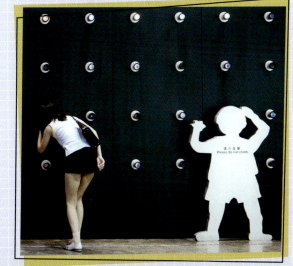

SONY EXPLORASCIENCE

RISUPIA

NERD WORD

YOU MAY HEAR THE TERM *OTAKU* TO MEAN AN OBSESSIVE GEEK OR NERD, INCLUDING PEOPLE WHO ARE INTO MANGA OR ANIME, AS WELL AS TECHNO-GEEKS.

GEEK CHIC

IN THE PAST, *OTAKU* WAS A NEGATIVE WORD AND QUITE RUDE, BUT TODAY IT'S BEEN RECLAIMED BY MANY GEEKS WHO HAPPILY USE THE WORD TO DESCRIBE THEMSELVES.

EVERYONE ELSE!

THERE'S NOW ANOTHER WORD, *RIAJUU*, WHICH DESCRIBES THE OPPOSITE OF *OTAKU* – OR EVERYONE ELSE! IT MEANS PEOPLE WHO ENJOY "LIVING LIFE TO THE FULLEST."

DO THE MATH

RISUPIA, ODAIBA

At this interactive science and math center in Odaiba, there are loads of cool games – including a digital tennis-style game where numbers fly towards you and split into smaller numbers when you hit the correct balls. As part of a showroom belonging to electrical giant Panasonic, there's also a display of electrical gadgets past and present.

TOKYO ON A PLATE

Wherever you go in Tokyo, food is not far away. The city has an incredible number of restaurants, cafés, and food stalls serving all kinds of Japanese specialties – as well as food from around the world, especially China and the US.

APPEARANCE IS AS IMPORTANT AS TASTE IN JAPANESE FOOD CULTURE. YOU'LL SEE FOOD IN ALL SORTS OF SHAPES, COLORS, AND ARRANGEMENTS.

START

ODAIBA TAKOYAKI MUSEUM

OCTOPUS BALLS

ODAIBA TAKOYAKI MUSEUM

This isn't really a museum, but more of a food theme park full of cafés selling varieties of the same thing – in this case, *takoyaki*. *Tako* is Japanese for "octopus," and *takoyaki* are little dumpling-like doughy balls filled with chopped, cooked octopus, and topped with sauce.

DIY PANCAKE

TSUKISHIMA

Tsukishima district is home to a local specialty: *monjayaki*, a kind of gloopy, fishy pancake. Diners have a grill at their table and cook the dish themselves. First, they fry some fillings, such as cabbage, cod roe (eggs), or eggplant. Then they add the runny, fish-flavored batter. The *monjayaki* never really sets, so, to eat it, you scrape it up with your own tiny spatula.

TSUKISHIMA

UNLIKE MOST JAPANESE FOOD, *MONJAYAKI* DOESN'T LOOK VERY NICE – IT'S EVEN BEEN SAID TO LOOK LIKE VOMIT!

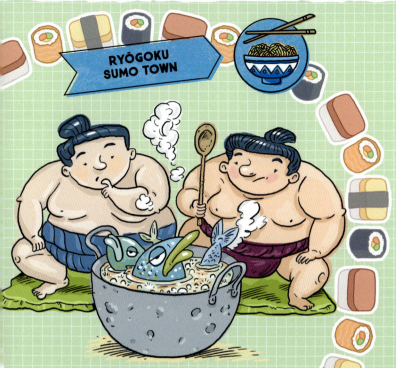

GOING CRACKERS!

TOKIWADO

Asakusa is the blast-from-the-past part of Tokyo, with lots of places selling traditional foods. At stores like Tokiwado, and nearby Iriyama Senbei, you can buy hundreds of varieties of *senbei*, or Japanese rice crackers, and even learn to make them yourself. The crunchy snacks can be sweet or savory, and come in endless flavors, colors, and designs – from leaf, tree, and animal shapes to hearts, discs with writing on them, and even mini-Mount Fujis.

DURING WORLD WAR II, JAPAN'S EMPEROR PRESENTED SPECIAL *SENBEI* TO HIS SUPPORTERS. EACH RICE CRACKER WAS STAMPED WITH A CHRYSANTHEMUM, THE JAPANESE ROYAL SYMBOL.

SUMO STEW

RYŌGOKU SUMO TOWN

Japan is famous for the ancient sport of sumo wrestling. Tokyo's Ryōgoku area is sumo central. As well as the sumo stadium and the sumo stables, where the wrestlers live and train, it also has lots of traditional sumo restaurants. They mainly serve *chanko nabe*, a high-calorie, high-protein meat or fish stew. Sumo wrestlers eat a large lunch of *chanko nabe* every day to help them gain weight, as this gives them an advantage. But anyone can visit and try the tasty stew for themselves.

88,000
RESTAURANTS AND CAFÉS

¥35·000 (US$320)
AVERAGE COST PER PERSON AT ARAGAWA – ONE OF TOKYO'S PRICIEST RESTAURANTS

1801
OPENING OF KOMAGATA DOZEU – THOUGHT TO BE TOKYO'S OLDEST RESTAURANT

NOODLE-OLOGY

SPEEDY CUISINE

Noodles are one of Tokyo's, and Japan's, favorite foods. They're long strings of dough that are cooked until they're soft and chewy. They can be made from wheat, rice, or other flour, mixed with water and sometimes eggs. They're quick to cook and eat – making them a perfect, cheap fast food.

SLUURRRP... IN JAPAN, SLURPING YOUR NOODLES IS THOUGHT TO MAKE THEM TASTE BETTER, SO IT'S NOT CONSIDERED RUDE.

PASTA FROM THE PAST

Noodles and their Italian cousin, pasta, are now both popular around the world – but noodles came first! They are thought to have originated in China as long as 4,000 years ago, and spread to Japan in medieval times.

NOODLES IN MOMENTS

Tokyo's noodle fans are especially fond of instant flavored noodles in a pot – called cup noodles or cup ramen. In fact, they have a museum dedicated to them! At the Cup Noodle Museum in Yokohama, besides discovering how inventor Momofuku Ando invented instant noodles, you can also design and make your own cup noodles recipe.

NOODLE CUISINE

NOT CONTENT WITH BRINGING INSTANT NOODLES TO THE WORLD, IN 2005, NOODLE SUPREMO MOMOFUKU ANDO ALSO DEVELOPED SPACE RAMEN – INSTANT NOODLES FOR USE BY ASTRONAUTS.

MMM... SAVORY!

Umami is one of the five basic flavors (including sweet, bitter, sour, salty) that our tongues can detect. It's a savory, salty, meaty flavor found in many dishes such as noodle soups.

NOODLE SOUP NEIGHBORHOOD

The Kanda district is home to a range of cafés selling *soba*, Tokyo's traditional noodle. You can have them as a posh dinner out, a quick form of fast food, and even for breakfast – either served on their own with a dipping sauce or in a hot, steamy noodle soup.

KNOW YOUR NOODLES!

SOBA
BROWN, NUTTY-TASTING, THIN, TRADITIONAL JAPANESE BUCKWHEAT NOODLES.

UDON
THICK, SOFT, CHEWY JAPANESE WHEAT NOODLES.

RAMEN
THIN, YELLOW, CHINESE-STYLE WHEAT AND EGG NOODLES.

search: DEPACHIKA

FREEBIES FOR FOODIES

Large department stores usually have a *depachika* (a gourmet food hall). A lot of the food is ultra-posh and expensive, but free samples are offered for shoppers to try. Specialty foods include things such as rare white strawberries, the finest *wagashi* (desserts), golden oysters, musk melons, and green tea.

KITCHEN SHOPPING

KAPPABASHI STREET

If you like cooking, Kappabashi Street has the best kitchenware, knives, pots, pans, serving bowls, and all the special equipment needed to make Japanese food. It's where Tokyo's thousands of chefs and restaurant owners go to stock up. The shops also sell every item of food imaginable – in fake form! Restaurants use this imitation food as decoration or to display their menus in their windows.

KAPPABASHI STREET

TOKYO DOME

TASTE OF THE TOWNS

TOKYO DOME

As if there aren't enough different foods to try in this city, every January in the Tokyo Dome Stadium there's a huge festival of food from around the country. It's called Furusato Matsuri (Festival of the Hometowns). Stalls from all over Japan sell all their local delicacies, and there's also a competition to make the best *donburi* dish (rice with a tasty topping).

HARAJUKU CRÊPE SHOPS

SWEET TREATS

HARAJUKU CRÊPE SHOPS

Ready for dessert? In Harajuku, home of everything bright, cheery, and colorful, shoppers keep their energy up with delicious crêpes – crispy pancakes stuffed with jam, whipped cream, marshmallows, fruit, chocolate sauce, or even pieces of cake. Some crêpe shops offer more than 100 varieties, and they all look stunning.

OMOIDE YOKOCHO

MEMORY LANE

OMOIDE YOKOCHO

This backstreet near Shinjuku station isn't where most tourists would want to head for a fancy meal – it's cramped, crowded, and rundown. But it's where people who like unusual traditional foods come. Why not try a grilled salamander, turtle hot pot, frog hearts, or some of the most personal parts of a pig?

Besides their own traditional snacks, the Japanese have adopted nibbles from all over the world, and they especially love potato chips. Visitors to Tokyo can find dozens of amazing flavors they've never heard of before, such as:

> SEAWEED > OCTOPUS
> PIZZA   > MILK
> THAI TOM YUM SOUP
> COD ROE (FISH EGG)
> COLA AND CHICKEN
> MANDARIN ORANGE
> WHITE CHOCOLATE

TOKYO STYLE

Whether it's a traditional flower-patterned silk kimono, the latest designer creation, or ever-changing Harajuku street style, you'll see endless striking and colorful outfits in Tokyo. Follow the trail and find out what to wear!

HIROSHI FUJIWARA IS A TOP TOKYO DJ, MUSIC PRODUCER, AND DESIGNER. CLOTHING COMPANIES FROM AROUND THE WORLD, SUCH AS NIKE, LEVI'S, AND CONVERSE, TURN TO HIM TO INJECT SOME CUTTING-EDGE TOKYO STREET STYLE INTO THEIR PRODUCTS.

START OMOTESANDŌ FLAGSHIP FASHION STORES

JAPANESE DESIGNERS OFTEN USE BOLD COLORS AND CREATE AMAZING MODERNIST STRUCTURAL SHAPES.

FLASH YOUR CASH

OMOTESANDŌ

This long, grand, tree-lined street connecting Harajuku to upmarket Aoyama is stuffed with the highest of high-end designer stores. There are super-posh brands from around the world, including Prada, Chanel, and Louis Vuitton, and also the flagship stores of Japan's own top designers, such as Yohji Yamamoto, Issey Miyake, and Rei Kawakubo.

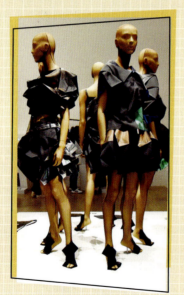

SKYSCRAPERS OF STYLE

FLAGSHIP FASHION STORES

International fashion houses, such as Tod's (seen right), have gone all out to build the most luxurious and dramatic shops you can imagine in classy Omotesandō. Check out these stunning temples to style, fashion, and glamour!

JAPANESE FASHION DESIGNERS ARE FAMOUS FOR THEIR FOLDED FABRIC CREATIONS — PERHAPS INSPIRED BY ORIGAMI, THE JAPANESE ART OF PAPER-FOLDING.

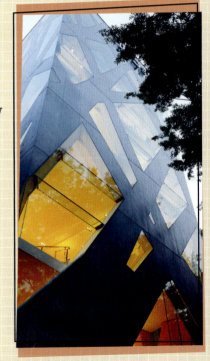

42

SHIBUYA

FASHION CITY

SHIBUYA 109, SHIBUYA

Nearby Shibuya is home to Shibuya 109, a department store with a famous tower. It's associated with *gyaru* (girl) and *kogal* (high school girl) fashion styles, based on childlike clothes or school uniforms, worn with baggy socks. Nearby, Fake Tokyo sounds like somewhere to buy an imitation designer handbag, but it's actually a store selling the work of the hottest new young fashion designers.

CUTTING-EDGE COOL

A BATHING APE, AOYAMA

One of Tokyo's wealthiest areas to live, Aoyama, is also home to some of the coolest street-style stores, such as A Bathing Ape. Like many other hip Japanese companies, it created its name using English words, though the phrase itself isn't familiar in English!

AOYAMA

MANY PEOPLE IN TOKYO WEAR MASKS OVER THEIR MOUTHS AND NOSES. THIS STARTED BECAUSE OF HEALTH SCARES ABOUT CITY SMOG AND FLU OUTBREAKS, BUT NOW SOME PEOPLE ALSO WEAR THEM AS A FASHION ACCESSORY. YOU'LL FIND THEM IN PATTERNS AND COLORS TO MATCH EVERY CLOTHING STYLE!

HIP HANGOUT

HARAJUKU DISTRICT

Close to Aoyama and Shibuya lies Harajuku, Tokyo's street fashion center. It has hundreds of fashion stores, but Harajuku isn't just about shopping – it's also about showing off! This is where hip teens and young adults strut their stuff in their latest outfits, and check out what everyone else is wearing. New trends spread like wildfire, only to be replaced by the next big thing just as fast.

THERE ARE NO RULES!

IN HARAJUKU, FASHION IS ABOUT FUN. TRENDS COME AND GO, BUT ANYONE CAN WEAR WHATEVER THEY LIKE. MIXING UP YOUR OWN CONCOCTION OF STYLES IS ALWAYS ADMIRED. LOOKS YOU MIGHT SPOT INCLUDE PUNK, GOTHIC, LOLITA, VICTORIAN, AND *GYARU* (GIRL), WITH MULTICOLORED CLOTHES, HAIR, NAILS, AND MAKE-UP.

POP PRINCESS OF STYLE

Pop singer and model Kyary Pamyu Pamyu is famous for her Harajuku style, and is seen as an ambassador for the area and its fashion. She was born Kiriko Takemura and grew up wearing Harajuku- and western-style outfits before becoming a blogger. Her full stage name is actually Caroline Charonplop Kyary Pamyu Pamyu, a name made up of Japanese versions of English names and words.

TAKE YOUR CAMERA

Tourists flock to Harajuku to go shopping and to see – and snap – the best street styles. Hangout spots such as Jingu Bashi, a bridge right next to Harajuku station, are the best places to spot them. You might see buskers and street dancers there, too, especially on Sundays. Some tourists even dress up themselves to stroll the Harajuku streets. When pointing a camera at someone, the Japanese use the phrase "*hai cheezu*" (say cheese).

ANOTHER POPULAR STYLE IS "COSPLAY," WHICH MEANS DRESSING AS AN ANIME OR MANGA CHARACTER.

search: HARAJUKU DISTRICT

SAMURAI VILLAGE
In medieval times, Harajuku was a village where samurai (Japanese knights) lived.

US SOLDIERS
During WWII (1939–1945), US soldiers were stationed in the area, and it became associated with western culture and shops.

TOKYO OLYMPICS
The Olympics were held in Tokyo in 1964, and many athletes stayed near Harajuku. This attracted crowds and made the area well-known.

HAPPENING HARAJUKU
The most famous fashion store in the area is LaForet Harajuku, which opened in 1978. It made the area a fashion destination, and other stores soon followed.

VINTAGE VIBES

SHIMOKITAZAWA

One station stop from glossy, gleaming Shibuya is the bohemian area of Shimokitazawa. In between looking seriously cool in cafés and browsing for old vinyl records along its narrow streets, you can find vintage and second-hand clothes for a hipster look.

KIMONO-SAKAEYA

GOING OLD STYLE

KIMONO SAKAEYA, HARAJUKU

Stepping back even further in time, Harajuku shop Kimono Sakaeya sells and rents out traditional Japanese kimonos. Besides helping you to try on these traditional robes and dress up in a full outfit, the staff will take you to a nearby park for photos, and serve you tea in a traditional ceremony as well.

WHAT'S A KIMONO?

THE KIMONO IS A LOOSE, T-SHAPED, ROBE-LIKE GARMENT, OFTEN MADE OF SILK, THAT'S BEEN WORN IN JAPAN SINCE ANCIENT TIMES, BY BOTH MEN AND WOMEN.

SOMETHING TO WEAR

THE NAME KIMONO SOUNDS PRETTY AND ARTISTIC, BUT SIMPLY MEANS "A THING TO WEAR" – FROM THE JAPANESE WORDS KI (WEAR) AND MONO (THING).

YUKATA

FEW PEOPLE WEAR FULL KIMONOS THESE DAYS, EXCEPT FOR WEDDINGS AND SPECIAL OCCASIONS. BUT MANY DO WEAR A YUKATA, A LIGHTWEIGHT DRESS-LIKE VERSION MADE OF COTTON, IN SUMMER.

SOU-SOU

OLD MEETS NEW

SOU-SOU, AOYAMA

This Aoyama store sells updated, colorful versions of traditional Japanese clothes – such as kimono-shaped dresses, as well as socks and shoes with two separate compartments for the big toe and the other toes, called *tabi*.

MAKE IT YOURSELF!

NIPPORI FABRIC DISTRICT

Budding fashion designers can source all the fabric they need from this fabric-stuffed shopping street. There's a huge home-sewing scene in Japan, and fabric designers, pattern designers, and sewing experts are celebrities among craft-lovers.

NIPPORI FABRIC DISTRICT

BEFORE MODERN STRETCHY FABRICS WERE INVENTED, JAPANESE MEN USED TO WEAR DIAPER–LIKE BAGGY COTTON UNDERWEAR, CALLED *FUNDOSHI*. TODAY, THEY'RE MAKING A COMEBACK, AND SOME WOMEN WEAR THEM, TOO – ESPECIALLY ON FUNDOSHI DAY, ON FEBRUARY 14. IN JAPANESE, THE PHRASE *FUNDOSHI O SHIMETE KAKARU* (TIGHTEN YOUR PANTS) IS USED TO MEAN "LET'S GET DOWN TO WORK!"

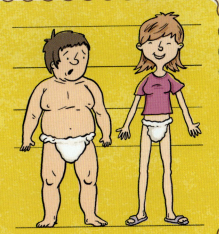

SPOOKY STORIES

Could this ultra-modern, hi-tech city really be heaving with horrible hauntings? The answer is yes! Japanese folklore is filled with strange spirits, ghosts, and ghouls, as well as plenty of scary urban myths – and Tokyo has lots of spooky spots and haunted corners.

SUNSHINE 60

 START

 HACHIŌJI

 INOKASHIRA PARK

CURSED SWAN BOATS

INOKASHIRA PARK

At nearby Inokashira Park, there's a beautiful boating lake, surrounded by cherry blossom trees, where you can hire a rowing boat, or even a pedal boat shaped like a swan. How romantic! But beware – the lake is said to be cursed by Benzaiten, the goddess of love, beauty, water, and words. She's said to be very jealous of lovers, and curses any couples who go for a boat ride, dooming them to split up.

WEEPING RUINS OF DORYO-DO

HACHIŌJI

To start your terrifying tour, head to Hachiōji in western Tokyo. Here, in the middle of Otukayama Park, lie the ruins of Doryo-do, an old temple. According to legend, two murders took place here, before the temple was destroyed. People have claimed to hear voices of the crying victims at night, wailing "I'm here, I'm here!" Yikes!

SCARY SKYSCRAPER

SUNSHINE 60

This skyscraper was built on the site of the notorious Sugamo Prison, where many criminals were executed. The new tower was given a nice, cheery name, but soon gained a reputation for being haunted. During construction, equipment broke down and several workers had mysterious accidents. Sunshine 60 is filled with shops, offices, cafés, and movie theaters, but people have reported hearing whispering, groaning, and rattling sounds, and seeing shadowy figures, spooky faces, and the ghost of an eyeless old woman who mumbles, "Where is it?"

60 THE NUMBER OF STORIES IN SUNSHINE 60

787 FT. (240 M)
THE SKYSCRAPER'S HEIGHT

1978 THE YEAR SUNSHINE 60 WAS COMPLETED

62 MILES (100 KM)
THE DISTANCE THAT YOU CAN SEE FROM THE TOP **ON A CLEAR DAY**

YUREI IZAKAYA GHOST BAR

SUNSHINE 60

SPOOKY SUPPER

YUREI IZAKAYA GHOST BAR

Literally meaning "ghost bar and restaurant," Yurei Izakaya is entirely decorated to look like a haunted house, echoing with scary music. The waiters are dressed as ghosts, and the food includes themed treats such as ghost intestines!

search: HAUNTED BATHROOMS

In Tokyo, as throughout Japan, people may enter bathrooms cautiously, thanks to the ghosts that are said to live there.

REIKO KASHIMA
This female ghost only has the upper part of her body, so she floats around bathrooms asking, "Where are my legs?"

HANAKO-SAN
This is a little girl ghost in a red dress, said to haunt school bathrooms – especially the third cubicle from the end.

AKANAME
Disgusting but mostly harmless, Akaname is a goblin-like creature who's said to hang around dirty bathrooms and lick them clean with his long tongue. Keep yours clean, or he might pay you a visit!

TALES TO MAKE YOU TREMBLE!

GHOST STORIES

Japanese folklore and legends are stuffed to the brim with terrifying ghost stories. *Yurei* (ghosts) also appear in many old artworks and dramas, and in modern manga cartoons and anime films, too. Some of these traditional tales are definitely just stories... while others are widely believed. Don't read this in the dark!

NIGHTMARE DOGS

Not all the ghosts in Japanese ghost stories are human. There are also many tales of scary *jinmenken* (ghost dogs) with human faces. They are said to race along roads at high speed, or skulk in dark areas at night. Many people have reported seeing one in the busy Shibuya district.

GHOST WITH A GRUDGE

The Oiwa-Inari Tamiya Shrine in Shinjuku is dedicated to Oiwa, the heroine of a famous Japanese ghost story. Oiwa was poisoned and pushed off a cliff by her husband, Iemon, so he could marry another woman, Oume. But Oiwa returned to haunt him. At his wedding to Oume, Oiwa's face appeared on Oume's body, and chased Iemon around. Finally, she forced him off the same cliff to his death. Though it's just a story, people still visit the shrine to pray for protection and keep curses away.

GHOST STORIES

BEWARE OF THE *NOPPERA-BŌ*

Kiinokuni Slope in the Akasaka district has a reputation as a scary spot, where people were petrified to set foot in the past. It was said to be haunted by a harmless yet totally terrifying type of Japanese ghost, the *noppera-bō*, which often features in scary stories. A *noppera-bō* looks like a normal person – often a young woman who seems to be sad or lonely. But when you approach, she turns towards you, revealing that she has no facial features, just smooth, blank skin. Aaaaaarrrgggh!

THE FLYING HEAD

TAIRA NO MASAKADO WAS A FAMOUS SAMURAI FROM THE KANTŌ REGION (WHICH INCLUDES TOKYO). HE FOUGHT AGAINST JAPAN'S RULERS AND WAS KILLED IN BATTLE IN THE YEAR 940. HIS HEAD WAS CUT OFF AND TAKEN TO KYOTO (JAPAN'S CAPITAL BACK THEN), TO BE PUT ON PUBLIC DISPLAY. LEGEND SAYS THAT THE HEAD DIDN'T ROT AWAY. ONE NIGHT, SO THE STORY GOES, IT FLEW BACK TO KANTŌ TO LOOK FOR ITS BODY. AFTER A FAILED SEARCH, IT LANDED NEAR TOKYO BAY, WHERE LOCALS BURIED IT. TODAY, THE MASAKADO SHRINE MARKS THE SPOT – AND IT'S SAID THAT THE SAMURAI'S SPIRIT CURSES ANYONE WHO TRIES TO DEMOLISH OR BUILD OVER IT.

DISAPPEAR HERE

SHINJUKU STATION MYSTERY CORRIDOR

It's one of the biggest and busiest train stations in the world (see page 70), so it's no surprise that Shinjuku station is easy to get lost in. But it could be even worse – you could disappear completely! A local legend says that somewhere among the dozens of corridors and platforms is a hidden underground tunnel that leads nowhere. If you accidentally wander into it... you'll never be seen again.

THE CREEPY SHINJUKU STATION CORRIDOR MAY OR MAY NOT REALLY EXIST – BUT THIS TERRIFYING GIANT EYE DEFINITELY DOES! THE GLASS ARTWORK, BY SCULPTOR YOKISHO MIYASHITA, STARES AT COMMUTERS FROM A WALL NEAR ONE OF THE STATION'S EXITS.

SHINJUKU STATION MYSTERY CORRIDOR

VAMPIRE CAFÉ

A BITE TO EAT

VAMPIRE CAFÉ

Tokyo's love of themed restaurants continues with the Vampire Café in the Ginza shopping district. Inside it looks like Dracula's castle, with coffins, candles, and bloodstains everywhere (even in the bathroom sinks!). The food is horror-themed, with a range of drinks that look like blood. Despite the dark decor, though, it's popular with shoppers, and usually full of people having fun.

HORROR MASKS

TOKYO NATIONAL MUSEUM

Stop off at the Tokyo National Museum to check out its collection of eerie-looking Noh masks. These are used in traditional Japanese Noh theater (see page 72) and come in all kinds of different characters and creatures, including ghosts, goblins, and demons.

↑
A FEMALE NOH MASK REPRESENTING CALMNESS AND PURITY

KAPPA-DERA TEMPLE

WATER GOBLINS

KAPPA-DERA TEMPLE, ASAKUSA

You really don't want to be grabbed by a kappa – a green, scaly, child-sized water creature. Kappas are said to leap out of ponds or rivers to scare people or drag them under. They have webbed hands and feet, and a hollow in the top of their heads, which they keep filled with water to give them their life force. To keep kappas happy, people leave offerings of cucumbers (thought to be their favorite food) at Kappa-Dera Temple. Here, you can see kappa statues and even a mummified arm that's said to have belonged to a kappa. Eww!

IT'S RATHER UNLIKELY, BUT IF YOU DID SEE A REAL KAPPA, WHAT SHOULD YOU DO? ACCORDING TO TRADITION, YOU CAN TRICK IT BY BOWING POLITELY. IT WILL THEN HAVE TO BOW BACK, THE WATER WILL FALL OFF ITS HEAD, AND IT WILL LOSE ITS LIFE-FORCE.

CARTOON CAPERS

Wherever you go in Tokyo, you'll see cartoons – or, to give them their Japanese names, anime (or animations) and manga (or comic books). They're closely related, as many of the most famous characters appear in both comics and cartoon movies or TV series. Some of them, such as Pokémon, and the movies of Studio Ghibli, are famous around the world.

START

SUGINAMI ANIMATION MUSEUM

FANTASY WORLD

GHIBLI MUSEUM, MITAKA

The most famous anime movies are probably those of Studio Ghibli. Movie fans around the world swoon over their delicately drawn characters and landscape. The magical stories combine nature and technology with Japanese folklore, spirits, and monsters. Meet them all at the studio's own museum, designed by legendary Ghibli director Hayao Miyazaki. The building resembles the castles and fairy-tale houses in his anime movies.

GHIBLI MUSEUM

LEARN THE BASICS

SUGINAMI ANIMATION MUSEUM

Many of Tokyo's manga and anime attractions are in the west of the city. The trail starts way out west in Suginami, at this fun museum all about the history of anime. There are exhibits by great anime and manga artists, interactive games that show how animation works, and light tables where you can draw your own animations. There's even a booth so you can record your own voiceovers to famous scenes.

search: ANIME

📍 ART ON FILM

Anime began in the early 1900s, soon after movie and cartoon animation were first invented in Europe and the US. Japanese artists wanted to develop their own movies and came up with an animation style that combined western cartoons with traditional Japanese art. Characters often have a recognizable, sharply drawn anime look, with big eyes and spiky hair.

CARTOONIFY YOURSELF!
PURIKURA-NO-MECCA

Purikura are photo booths where you not only take photos of yourself and your friends, but edit your pictures, too, adding slogans, hair colors, make-up, cute stickers, and so on. At this *purikura* mall, the machines will help you make an anime-style version of yourself, by enlarging your eyes to look like an anime or manga character. You can even get dressed up first!

SHIROHIGE'S CREAM PUFF FACTORY

PURIKURA-NO-MECCA

CARTOON CAKE
SHIROHIGE'S CREAM PUFF FACTORY

On the way back into town, stop at Shirohige's Cream Puff Factory to enjoy a cream puff shaped like Totoro – one of the most popular characters in Japanese animation. Borrowed from French cuisine, cream puffs are hugely popular in Japan – soft pastry on the outside, filled with cream, custard, and other yummy flavorings.

OUTSIDE THE TOKYO HEADQUARTERS OF TV COMPANY NTV, THERE'S A GINORMOUS CLOCK CALLED THE NI-TELE REALLY BIG CLOCK. DESIGNED BY HAYAO MIYAZAKI, ITS WOODLAND-THEMED CARTOON STYLE CONTRASTS WITH THE SURROUNDING SKYSCRAPERS. EVERY FEW HOURS, IT MARKS THE TIME WITH MUSIC, BELLS, AND 3D MECHANICAL MOVEMENTS, WATCHED BY CROWDS OF ONLOOKERS.

MANGA MURALS
TAKADANOBABA STATION

A wall next to this station is decorated with an enormous, colorful mural of manga art, celebrating the work of Osamu Tezuka, one of the most influential manga and anime artists of all time. Born in 1928, Tezuka was inspired to become a manga and anime artist by Disney cartoons from the US. In the 1950s, he pioneered the big-eyed manga drawing style. He's most famous for his android character Astro Boy (or Mighty Atom), who features in the murals here.

OSAMU TEZUKA PRODUCED A VAST AMOUNT OF MATERIAL

700 MANGA COMICS

500 ANIME EPISODES

150,000 PAGES OF MANGA ARTWORK

J-WORLD TOKYO

SHONEN THEME PARK
J-WORLD TOKYO

Shonen is manga aimed at teenage boys, with cartoon series such as *One Piece*, *Naruto*, and *Dragon Ball-Z*. At indoor manga theme park J-World, there are *shonen*-themed rides, interactive role-playing games, video game machines, and 3D re-creations. If you're a reader of best-selling manga magazine *Weekly Shonen Jump*, you'll LOVE J-World. If you're not, you might be a bit confused!

WHO'S YOUR FAVORITE?
CHARACTER STREET

Can't decide which cartoon character you love most? There's a choice of hundreds of them on Character Street, an underground shopping corridor located in the basement of Tokyo's main train station. From Pokémon, Ghibli characters, and manga stars, to Hello Kitty, Doraemon, Miffy, and the Moomins, the stores sell merchandise featuring cartoons from Japan and around the world.

POCKET MONSTERS
POKÉMON CENTER

The Pokémon cartoon concept began life as a computer game in 1995. It has now extended into manga and anime series, trading cards, full-length movies, books, toys, and merchandise. Everything Pokémon-themed you can possibly think of can be found at the Pokémon Center – Japan's biggest Pokémon store. But what are Pokémon? Short for "pocket monsters," they're cute, animal-like cartoon creatures. There are over 700 "species" in total, each with its own features and fighting powers. The aim of the game is to collect Pokémon and train them for competitions.

POKÉMON CREATOR AND VIDEO GAME DESIGNER, SATOSHI TAJIRI, LOVED COLLECTING INSECTS AS A CHILD. HE BASED THE CONCEPT FOR POKÉMON ON THIS HOBBY.

AMAZING ART

If you like awesome art, Tokyo's a great place to be. Not only can you visit countless art galleries and museums – you're also likely to stumble across amazing public artworks, sculptures, murals, and arty graffiti every time you turn a corner.

ARCHITECT KISHO KUROKAWA SAID HE WANTED TO MAKE THE NATIONAL ART CENTER FEEL CONFUSING AND "FUZZY" FOR VISITORS, AS IF THEY WERE IN A MAZE.

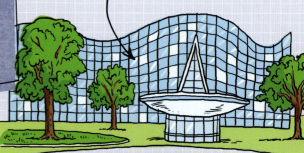

START

TARŌ OKAMOTO MEMORIAL MUSEUM

NATIONAL ART CENTER

ART IS EXPLOSION!
TARŌ OKAMOTO MEMORIAL MUSEUM

Tokyo has been home to many great artists past and present, and, in Japan, Tarō Okamoto is one of the most famous. He loved to challenge both traditional and modern ideas about art, and is famous for his expression: "Art is explosion!" After traveling the world, Tarō returned to Tokyo in the 1950s. His old home in Aoyama had been destroyed in World War II, so he built a new house and studio in the same place. Today, you can visit it and see his studio just as it was when he worked there, as well as lots of his wacky and colorful sculptures.

GARGANTUAN GALLERY
NATIONAL ART CENTER

This huge art gallery, one of many galleries in the Roppongi area, opened in 2007. It is the biggest exhibition space in Japan. As well as the art, people visit just to see the beautiful building, created by architect Kisho Kurokawa, with its breathtaking, wave-shaped glass front. The gallery doesn't have any permanent shows. Instead, it hosts an ever-changing variety of exhibitions by great Japanese and international artists and designers, such as Salvador Dali, Issey Miyake, Paul Cezanne, and Yayoi Kusama.

IN THE 1960S, TARŌ OKAMOTO WENT TO MEXICO, WHERE HE WORKED ON A HUGE MURAL FOR A MEXICAN HOTEL LOBBY. BUT WHEN THE HOTEL COULDN'T PAY FOR IT, IT GOT LEFT BEHIND IN A WAREHOUSE, AND WAS LOST FOR OVER 30 YEARS. AFTER TARŌ DIED IN 1996, HIS FAMILY REDISCOVERED THE MURAL AND HAD IT BROUGHT TO TOKYO.

TOKYO-BASED ARTIST YAYOI KUSAMA IS FAMOUS FOR HER PAINTINGS, SCULPTURES, INSTALLATIONS, AND FASHION DESIGNS FEATURING ENDLESS SPOTS.

 TENNOZU ISLE

ART ISLAND

TENNOZU ISLE

Tiny Tennozu Isle, near Tokyo Harbor, used to be a bit gray and dull-looking, as it's mostly full of offices, factories, and warehouses. In 2015, to liven it up, street artists were invited to cover it in murals and sculptures for a street art festival. Many of the artworks are still there, turning the island into an outdoor art gallery.

TOKYO MIDTOWN

WHAT SHAPE IS YOUR MIND?

TOKYO MIDTOWN

In between shopping, eating, and sightseeing at this fancy modern development, you can admire *Shape of Mind* and *Key to a Dream*, by sculptor Kan Yasuda. Luckily, you're allowed to touch these sculptures! People just can't resist their smooth surfaces, and they're usually surrounded by children.

THE GREAT MASTER

KATSUSHIKA HOKUSAI

There's one work of Japanese art that's famous around the world, and is better-known than any other. It's this picture – *The Great Wave Off Kanagawa*. It's a woodblock print made around 1830 by the great Tokyo artist Katsushika Hokusai. In the image, a terrifying wave towers over open boats as their crews huddle inside, with majestic Mount Fuji on the shore in the distance.

PEOPLE OFTEN JUST CALL THE PICTURE "THE GREAT WAVE" OR "THE WAVE."

RESTING PLACE

Hokusai is buried in Tokyo, at the small Seikyo-ji temple in Asakusa. His grave has a statue of him on top, and is inscribed with the last name he used, Gakyo Rojin Manji. It roughly translates as "the old man who's crazy about art."

HOKUSAI MUSEUM

For Hokusai fans, and anyone who wants to find out more about him, the Sumida Hokusai Museum is a must-see. It opened in 2016 in Sumida, Tokyo, where Hokusai was born in 1760. Besides *The Great Wave* and many other artworks, the museum has exhibits showing what Tokyo was like in Hokusai's lifetime. There's also a re-creation of his workshop, with robot versions of Hokusai and his daughter Oei, who was also an artist.

WHO AM I?

Like many artists of his time, Hokusai often changed his name to reflect his stage of life and what he was working on. As a child, he was called Tokitaro, and during his lifetime, he had over 30 other names! The one we use today is made up of Katsushika, the local area he was born in, and Hokusai, which means "north studio."

70-YEAR CAREER

THOUGH HE'S BEST KNOWN FOR ONE GREAT WORK, HOKUSAI DID A LOT MORE BESIDES. FROM THE AGE OF 18 UNTIL HIS DEATH AT AGE 88, HE WORKED ALMOST CONSTANTLY, MAKING PRINTS, PAINTING, DRAWING, AND WRITING BOOKS ABOUT ART. HE WAS NEVER QUITE HAPPY WITH HIS WORK, AND ALWAYS WANTED TO IMPROVE. WHEN HE WAS ABOUT TO DIE, HE REPORTEDLY MOANED: "IF ONLY HEAVEN WILL GIVE ME JUST ANOTHER TEN YEARS... JUST FIVE MORE YEARS, THEN I COULD BECOME A REAL PAINTER!"

SAW, SAWING

TOKYO BIG SIGHT

By the harbor, in the grounds of Tokyo Big Sight (Tokyo International Exhibition Center), is a humongous saw, stuck in the ground! The sculpture, by European artists Claes Oldenburg and Coosje van Bruggen, is 50 ft. (15 m) tall and made of steel, resin, and plastic. It looms over passersby at a steep angle. But don't worry, it's been built to withstand Japan's earthquakes.

"Anyone seen my saw?"

HANDS ON

MUSEUM OF CONTEMPORARY ART

This gallery in a super-modern building is packed with modern art from Japan and around the world. It also has activities and workshops, so you can try all kinds of art techniques yourself, as well as exhibitions for children, where they can touch and climb on artworks.

MUSEUM OF CONTEMPORARY ART

62

SHUTTER SHOW

ASAKUSA

As a way to glam up the busy Asakusa shopping district, many of the rolling shutters used to secure the shops have been painted with traditional Japanese art. You have to wait until the evening, when the shops close and pull their shutters down, to get a good look at them. They include versions of woodblock prints and scenes from traditional Kabuki theater and dances.

MODERN SHOP SHUTTERS ARE MADE OF METAL, BUT THEY UNFURL DOWNWARDS SIMILAR TO THE OLD PAPER OR SILK SCROLLS TRADITIONALLY USED FOR JAPANESE PAINTINGS. THEY WERE STORED ROLLED UP, AND USED AT SPECIAL OCCASIONS SUCH AS FESTIVALS.

ASAKUSA

3331 ARTS CHIYODA

JOIN IN!

3331 ARTS CHIYODA

This art center is aimed at children and families, with loads of activities to enjoy. In its children's play area, thousands of old toys have been recycled to make gigantic art patterns and huge, roaring dinosaur sculptures.

WHY "3331"? THIS NAMES COMES FROM A JAPANESE HAND-CLAPPING CUSTOM CALLED *TEJIME*. IN THE TOKYO VERSION, *EDO IPPON TEJIME*, YOU CLAP YOUR HANDS THREE TIMES, ANOTHER THREE TIMES, ANOTHER THREE TIMES AND THEN ONE FINAL TIME — WHILE SHOUTING "IYO'O!" WHICH MEANS SOMETHING LIKE "HURRAH!" PEOPLE DO THIS TO CELEBRATE SOMETHING TOGETHER.

24-HOUR TOKYO

They say New York is "the city that never sleeps," but Tokyo has an equally good claim to that title. There's so much going on at night, people never run out of things to do... even if they can't get to sleep!

JAPAN HAS VENDING MACHINES FOR ALMOST EVERYTHING, AND IN TOKYO THEY'RE EVERYWHERE. IF YOU CAN'T FIND A SHOP THAT'S STILL OPEN, A MACHINE MAY HAVE JUST WHAT YOU NEED. THINGS YOU CAN BUY FROM THEM INCLUDE:

- **SOCKS**
- **T-SHIRTS**
- **TIES**
- **SHOES**
- **CAMERAS**
- **PET FOOD**
- **BREAD**
- **EGGS**
- **UMBRELLAS**
- **FRESH FLOWERS**
- **FRUITS AND VEGGIES**
- **MAGGOTS FOR FISHING**
- **LIVE LOBSTERS**

SO, WHAT DO YOU WANT?

START ★★★ → KARAOKE KAN, SHIBUYA

SING YOUR HEART OUT

KARAOKE KAN, SHIBUYA

Karaoke is a Japanese invention that's spread all over the world. It involves singing along to a pop music track with the vocals removed, to show off your own performance skills.

THE WORD KARAOKE MEANS "EMPTY ORCHESTRA."

Tokyo is full of karaoke bars, where groups of friends can reserve a special room and a karaoke machine, and take turns singing late into the night. Karaoke Kan is one of the most famous (it featured in the film *Lost in Translation*) and it stays open until 6:00 a.m. Don't worry if you're out of tune... no one minds!

BUY ANYTHING

SHINJUKU

Many areas of Tokyo are busy at night, but Shinjuku is the most wide-awake of them all. Here, you'll find cafés, restaurants, bookstores, theaters, and clubs that stay open all hours, and streets almost as busy as they are during the day. If you need anything (and we mean ANYTHING), head to a branch of the variety store Don Quijote, also known as Donki. It's piled high with everything you can think of – snacks, clothes, make-up, electronic gadgets, tools... or even a new suitcase to put your purchases in.

SHINJUKU ★★★ →

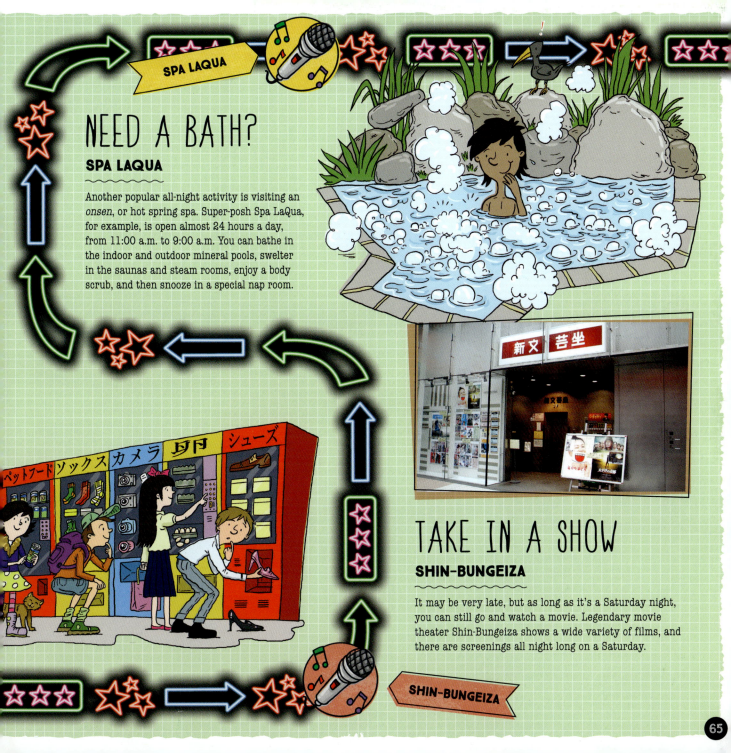

NEED A BATH?

SPA LAQUA

Another popular all-night activity is visiting an *onsen*, or hot spring spa. Super-posh Spa LaQua, for example, is open almost 24 hours a day, from 11:00 a.m. to 9:00 a.m. You can bathe in the indoor and outdoor mineral pools, swelter in the saunas and steam rooms, enjoy a body scrub, and then snooze in a special nap room.

TAKE IN A SHOW

SHIN-BUNGEIZA

It may be very late, but as long as it's a Saturday night, you can still go and watch a movie. Legendary movie theater Shin-Bungeiza shows a wide variety of films, and there are screenings all night long on a Saturday.

SPA LAQUA

SHIN-BUNGEIZA

ALL-NIGHT AMUSEMENTS

LEISURELAND

Feel like a nighttime game of ping-pong, pool, bowling, or darts? Leisureland, a vast amusement arcade in Odaiba, has all this and more available 24 hours a day. There are arcade games, robots for children to ride, sports, and karaoke. You can even go fishing in an indoor pond, or visit a fairground-style haunted house. Perfect for the middle of the night!

LEISURELAND

search: LIGHT ARCHITECTURE

BRIGHT-LIGHT CITY
The night is bright in Tokyo, thanks to the many buildings and structures that are decorated with patterns of colored lights, also known as "light architecture."

RAINBOW BRIDGE
The famous Rainbow Bridge, linking Odaiba to the mainland, was named by the public, and lives up to the name with its multicolored, solar-powered light architecture.

TOKYO TOWER
The landmark orange-and-white pointed tower has a range of nighttime colors.

TOKYO GATE BRIDGE
This angular bridge reflects its modern style with icy-white night lighting.

LOTTE KASAI GOLF

DRIVING IN THE DARK

LOTTE KASAI GOLF

It might seem like an especially crazy thing to do in the dark, but yes, you really can play golf all night in Tokyo. Lotte Kasai Golf driving range near Tokyo Bay is lit up with bright floodlights.

"It's over there!"

"No, it went that way!"

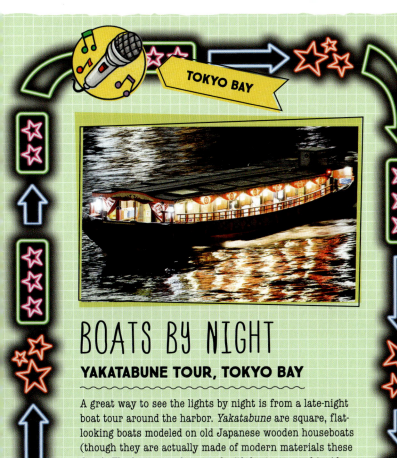

BOATS BY NIGHT

YAKATABUNE TOUR, TOKYO BAY

A great way to see the lights by night is from a late-night boat tour around the harbor. *Yakatabune* are square, flat-looking boats modeled on old Japanese wooden houseboats (though they are actually made of modern materials these days). The boats are decorated with lanterns, and inside they look like an old-fashioned Japanese house. While you goggle at the illuminations, you can also graze on traditional Japanese snacks, such as deep-fried fish or vegetable tempura.

FLOWERS AT DAWN

OTA MARKET

At 5:00 a.m., when the clubs and karaoke bars start to close, the enormous Ota Market opens up its doors. Traders come here to stock up on fresh fruits, vegetables, and flowers. Visitors are welcome, too. Tourists can stroll along a special walkway to view the auctions from above.

CLOSE TO OTA MARKET IS SEASIDE PARK, NEXT TO TOKYO BAY. IT'S A GREAT PLACE TO WATCH THE SUN RISE. JAPAN IS OFTEN CALLED "THE LAND OF THE RISING SUN," A NAME REFLECTED IN THE COUNTRY'S FLAG.

AS ONE OF THE WORLD'S BIGGEST AND MOST MODERN CITIES, TOKYO IS A BLAZE OF LIGHT BY NIGHT, EVEN WHEN SEEN FROM SPACE!

OTA MARKET

BUSY AND NOISY!

Once upon a time, where Tokyo stands now, there was nothing but a tiny, peaceful fishing village called Edo. Fast-forward a thousand years or so, and it's one of the biggest, busiest cities in the world. And it's not just busy – it's also very LOUD! Residents are used to crowds, crushes, and lots of noise, but visitors can be in for a shock...

38 MILLION POPULATION OF GREATER TOKYO AREA

16,000 NUMBER OF PEOPLE PER SQ. MILE

882 NUMBER OF RAILWAY AND SUBWAY STATIONS IN TOKYO AREA

START

SENSŌ-JI TEMPLE

SHOPPING CENTRAL

GINZA

Ginza is Tokyo's ultimate shopping district, full of designer clothes outlets, grand department stores, and cafés. On Saturdays, it's so busy that the main street through Ginza is closed to traffic, to make space for shoppers. It's also known as Hokosha Tengoku, or "pedestrian heaven."

FESTIVAL FRENZY

SENSŌ-JI TEMPLE

This ancient Buddhist temple is thought to date from the year AD 628 – which makes it older than Tokyo itself. It's a major tourist attraction, so the streets around here are always packed with tourists, temple-goers, and shoppers. But on the third weekend in May, it's even more of a squeeze, as the massive Sanja Matsuri festival takes over, the streets are closed to carts, and over a million people come to watch or take part. The festival honors the spirits of the three men who founded the Sensō-Ji temple. It features music, dancing, and noisy parades of *mikoshi* (miniature portable shrines) through the streets.

GINZA

3, 2, 1 CROSS!

SHIBUYA CROSSING

Each time the lights change at this intersection next to Shibuya Station, up to 1,000 people surge across, weaving in and out and dodging each other as they head in numerous different directions. In a day, it's thought that up to a million people use Shibuya Crossing (also known as Shibuya Scramble), making it one of the busiest on the planet. While it's fun to have a go at making it across yourself, many people prefer to sit and watch from one of the many cafés around the crossing.

TOKYO'S BUSIEST AREAS ARE FILLED WITH HUGE BILLBOARDS, NEON SIGNS, AND ELECTRONIC LIT-UP MESSAGES THAT SCROLL ACROSS THE FRONT OF LARGE BUILDINGS. NOT ONLY THAT — MANY OF THE ADS ARE VIDEOS WITH SOUND INCLUDED, WHICH TALK TO YOU AS YOU WALK PAST.

I LOVE MY WIFE!

HIBIYA PARK

Strangely, although Tokyo is so busy and noisy, Japanese people are often quite reserved. It's considered polite to be quiet on trains and in shops, for example (unless you're the shop owner yelling out the door for potential customers!). And people don't normally express their feelings out loud in public. So, on January 31 every year, there's a special event in Hibiya Park, where men can use a microphone to announce to the world how much they love their wife – usually screaming it as loudly as they can! Women can take part, too, and the announcements are shown on TV.

WHEN YOU WALK INTO A SHOP, STAFF MEMBERS ARE ALL LIKELY TO SHOUT "IRASSHAIMASE!" WHICH MEANS "WELCOME!" IT'S SEEN AS GOOD CUSTOMER SERVICE TO GREET YOU AS WARMLY AS POSSIBLE.

HIBIYA PARK

SHINJUKU STATION

IT'S TIRING STRIKING A GIANT BELL OVER AND OVER AGAIN, SO AT NEW YEAR, TEMPLE VISITORS ARE OFTEN INVITED TO DO SOME RINGING THEMSELVES (SEE BELOW).

BONGGGGG!

ZŌJŌ-JI TEMPLE

Zōjō-Ji, near the Tokyo Tower, is another very old traditional Buddhist temple. It's home to Daibonsho, a massive bronze bell made in 1673, which is rung twice a day. The bell-ringing goes up a notch every New Year's Eve, though. On this night, the Daibonsho, and other temple bells around Japan, are rung 108 times, in a special ceremony called Joya no Kane (New Year's Eve Bell-Ringing).

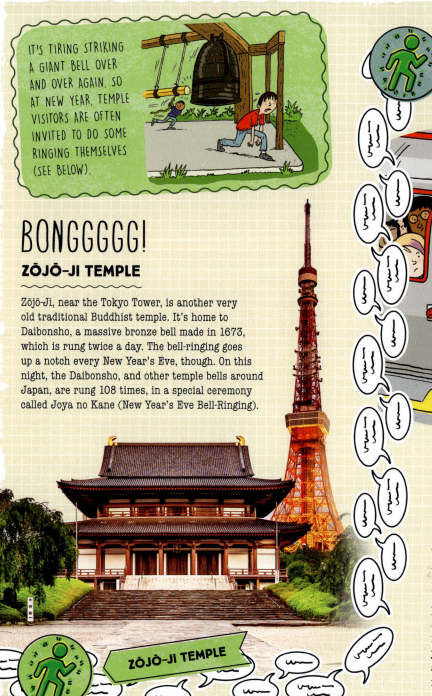

ZŌJŌ-JI TEMPLE

SO MANY TRAINS

SHINJUKU STATION

Alhough it's not right in the middle of Tokyo, Shinjuku is the city's busiest train station. In fact, it's the world's busiest station, with well over 3 million passengers passing through it every day. Multiple subway and aboveground railway lines meet here, and the station is SO complicated that even looking at a map of it hurts your brain! It's noisy, too – besides all the passengers and trains, there are constant announcements and musical jingles played over loudspeakers.

PACHINKO!

MARUHAN PACHINKO

It sounds noisy, and it is – *pachinko* is a pinball-type game, and each *pachinko* machine is filled with tiny steel balls that rattle around at high speed. Near Shinjuku is the Maruhan *pachinko* parlor – one of many dotted around Tokyo. Maruhan can hold more than 700 people playing the game at the same time – imagine the racket!

MARUHAN PACHINKO

search: SOUNDS OF TOKYO

MANY DIFFERENT NOISES MAKE UP THE NONSTOP SOUNDS OF TOKYO LIFE:

- Loud video billboards.
- Endless digging, building, and maintenance work.
- Shop and stall owners describing their wares, sometimes using megaphones.
- Public loudspeaker announcements.
- Trains rumbling overhead on elevated railway tracks.
- Crosswalks, traffic lights, and station platforms that beep, talk, or play tunes.

BZZZZZZZZZZZZ!!!

PARKS AND AVENUES

Besides all these noises, in summer you'll often hear something that sounds like a circular saw or a loud, high-pitched electrical buzz. But when you look around, there are no machines or workers to be seen. It's actually a natural sound – the mating call of the cicada, a large scary-looking, but harmless, insect. The males make the noise, not by buzzing their wings but by vibrating special drum-like parts on the sides of their bodies.

WHEN THE TREES ARE FULL OF CICADAS, IT CAN BE SO LOUD YOU CAN'T HAVE A CONVERSATION!

ACTUAL SIZE!

PARKS AND AVENUES

ON WITH THE SHOW!

Every kind of entertainment is available in Tokyo, from 600-year-old traditional theater to monster movies, puppet shows, and J-pop singing troupes. Grab some tickets and take the theater trail!

START

NATIONAL NOH THEATRE

NOH!

NATIONAL NOH THEATRE

Noh! That's what some people say when they're invited to an evening of this 600-year-old form of drama. It is often seen as a bit dull and hard to understand. It features actors in masks, performing a mixture of traditional dance, song, and comedy in old-fashioned Japanese – and it tends to go on for a long time. But recently, Noh has been made more appealing, with shorter shows and the first-ever female Noh actors (they used to be all male). Even if you're not sure what's going on, a Noh show is a colorful spectacle.

IN THE PAST, NOH WAS PERFORMED OUTDOORS ON A HUT-LIKE OPEN WOODEN STAGE WITH A ROOF. THE NATIONAL NOH THEATRE HAS RE-CREATED THIS TYPE OF STAGE, BUT INSIDE A LARGER BUILDING (SO YOU CAN KEEP WARM WHILE WATCHING!).

SHOWS TO SEE FOR FREE

YOYOGI PARK

Close to the hip Harajuku district, there's almost always some kind of show or event happening at Yoyogi Park. Besides bigger festivals and performances, you can see creative types practicing their dancing, juggling, mime, or traditional Japanese drumming. And on Sundays, Elvis Presley impersonators gather to enjoy a 1950s-style dance-off!

YOYOGI PARK

IS THAT A MONSTER?

SHINJUKU GRACERY HOTEL

There is a monster leaning over the roof of the Shinjuku Gracery Hotel. It's Godzilla, a dinosaur-like creature from a famous series of Japanese films, in which the massive monster rampages through Tokyo. The hotel even has a Godzilla-themed room with a huge monster claw over the bed. Godzilla isn't really scary, though – he's a much-loved icon of Japanese cinema, and is seen as quite cute, or even heroic. Further out of the city, to the west, Toho Studios, where the original Godzilla films were made in the 1950s, has more monster-themed statues and attractions.

LIVING PUPPETS

NATIONAL THEATRE OF JAPAN

You've never seen a puppet show like this! Japanese traditional puppet theater, or *Bunraku*, is performed at the National Theatre of Japan for several weeks every year – and it's a mind-blowing sight. Each puppet is operated by up to three puppeteers dressed in black, who take many years to train. The puppets themselves are mechanical marvels, with moving parts operated by handles and levers – they can even change their facial expressions. The result is eerily lifelike.

TOKYO TAKARAZUKA THEATRE

STAGE SPECTACULAR
KABUKIZA THEATRE

This is the place to go to watch *Kabuki*, the most popular type of traditional Japanese theater. It's an exciting experience, with fights and dances, dramatic music, stunning sets and costumes, amazing make-up, and comical slapstick and acrobatics. The actors are usually all male, with men playing female parts, and the best female impersonators can become huge stars. It was the other way around when *Kabuki* first began — all the parts were played by women, just like in the all-girl Takarazuka company.

UNLIKE NOH THEATER, KABUKI THEATER WAS ORIGINALLY CREATED FOR THE COMMON PEOPLE, AND ITS MANY PERFORMANCES PORTRAY HISTORICAL EVENTS FROM JAPAN'S PAST.

KABUKIZA THEATRE

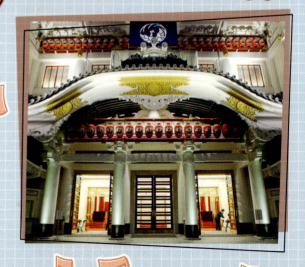

PERFECT PARTNERS
TOKYO TAKARAZUKA THEATRE

The unique Takarazuka Revue is an all-woman theater group, started over 100 years ago by a railway company, that puts on glamorous, all-singing, all-dancing romantic musicals. It sounds bizarre, but the shows are hugely popular. The troupe began in the town of Takarazuka, but have a theater in Tokyo, too. It's mostly women who go to watch the shows — they're said to be impressed by the romantic male lead characters, who are seen as perfect men! They're actually played by female actors called *otokoyaku*.

OIWAKE, ASAKUSA

J-POP IDOLS

AKIHABARA

You've heard of boy bands and girl groups — but the Japanese take them to a whole new level! Singing troupe Kamen Joshi (meaning "masked girls") has 18 members, while AKB48 has over 100 (though they do take turns performing). The groups have their own theaters in the Akihabara district, where they perform J-pop, or Japanese pop music, almost every day. Pop stars like these are known as "idols" and are expected to behave like role models for their millions of fans.

search: TRADITIONAL JAPANESE INSTRUMENTS

SOUNDS JAPANESE

The well-known haunting, twanging sound of Japanese music is thanks to a special set of traditional instruments:

📍 **SHAMISEN**
A banjo-like instrument with three strings, plucked with the fingers or with a tool called a *bachi*.

📍 **SHAKUHACHI**
The traditional five-holed bamboo flute of Japan.

📍 **TAIKO**
Various types of drums, beaten with thick wooden sticks.

SOUNDS OF THE PAST

OIWAKE, ASAKUSA

Most cities have an old pub or bar where you can go to see live traditional folk music. In Tokyo, head to Oiwake, in the Asakusa district. There are performances of traditional music and songs (*minyo*) every day, played by musicians who also work at the bar.

TO PERFORM, THE OIWAKE PLAYERS WEAR UNIFORMS CALLED HAPPI COATS.

TICKET TO RIDE

Tokyo is a massive place with millions of people, and it takes a LOT of trains, trams, buses, and boats to get everyone around. This being Japan, they happen to include some of the fastest and most futuristic vehicles on the planet.

4,000+ TRAINS SET OFF FROM **TOKYO STATION** EVERY SINGLE DAY

3 BILLION+ PASSENGERS PER YEAR USE TOKYO'S RAIL AND SUBWAY SYSTEMS

1,243+ MILES (2,000+ KM) OF TRACK CRISSCROSS THE GREATER TOKYO AREA

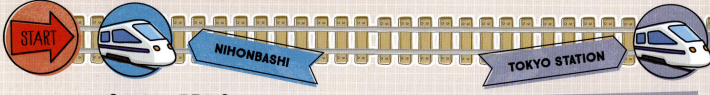

START · NIHONBASHI · TOKYO STATION

POINT ZERO

NIHONBASHI

Let's start at the very beginning, on Nihonbashi. This old bridge across the Nihonbashi River is officially the center point of Tokyo, and it's where all road distances to other parts of the country are measured from. The bridge is decorated with bronze dragons and lions, and in the middle there's a bronze plaque marking "kilometer zero," the central point.

AT RUSH HOUR, TOKYO TRAINS GET SO BUSY THAT STATIONS EMPLOY *OSHIYA* (TRAIN PUSHERS). THEIR JOB IS TO CRAM PASSENGERS INTO THE PACKED TRAINS SO THAT THE DOORS CAN CLOSE AND THE TRAIN CAN LEAVE ON TIME.

ZOOM AWAY

TOKYO STATION

Not far away from Nihonbashi district is Tokyo's main train station. Although Shinjuku station has the most passengers, Tokyo station has more trains, linking the city to all the other parts of Japan. The roof garden of the Kitte Shopping Mall next door is a good place to watch the trains from. Not into trainspotting? You'll still want to catch a glimpse of a *shinkansen*, or bullet train – an ultra-sleek, ultra-fast intercity train.

COOL CRUISER

HIMIKO WATER TAXI

Tokyo is on the coast and also has lots of rivers, so a water bus is another great way to get around the city. The boat to catch is the *Himiko*, which carries passengers up and down the Sumida River, between Asakusa and Odaiba. Designed by manga artist Leiji Matsumoto, it looks like something out of a sci-fi movie.

HIMIKO WATER TAXI

A VIEW FROM THE BRIDGE

RAINBOW BRIDGE

Connecting mainland Tokyo to the many offshore islands in Tokyo Bay is the beautiful Rainbow Bridge. It was built to multi-task, with an eight-lane expressway on the top, a railway line underneath, and two passenger walkways, one on each side.

2,618 FT.
TOTAL LENGTH

413 FT. HEIGHT

1987
CONSTRUCTION BEGAN

AUGUST 26, 1993
BRIDGE OPENED

RAINBOW BRIDGE

CARS OF THE FUTURE

TOKYO BIG SIGHT

Besides all its public transportation systems, Tokyo has a LOT of roads and cars, as well as several big car companies. Every two years, these companies (and other carmakers from around the world) show off their latest models and designs at the massive Tokyo Motor Show, held at Tokyo Big Sight. Visitors get to check out — and sit in — the coolest futuristic space-age cars, green machines, and self-driving vehicles.

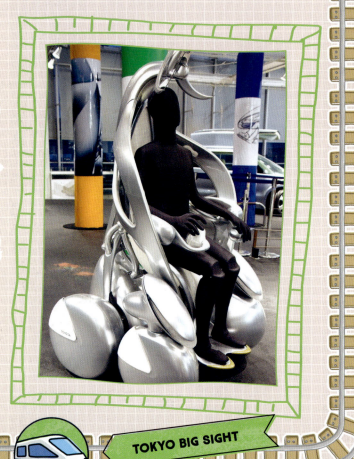

TOKYO METRO MUSEUM

UNDERGROUND ADVENTURE

TOKYO METRO MUSEUM

The Tokyo subway, or underground train network, is the world's busiest, carrying over 3 BILLION passengers per year. Train lovers can find out all about it at this museum in the east of the city. There are old subway trains, a re-creation of the city's first subway station (opened in 1927), a section of subway tunnel, and simulators so you can try driving the trains yourself.

TOKYO BIG SIGHT

WHEN TRAVELING ON THE TOKYO SUBWAY, REMEMBER NOT TO USE YOUR PHONE! IT'S FROWNED UPON TO DISTURB YOUR FELLOW PASSENGERS BY HAVING A LONG CHAT OR PLAYING A VIDEO GAME.

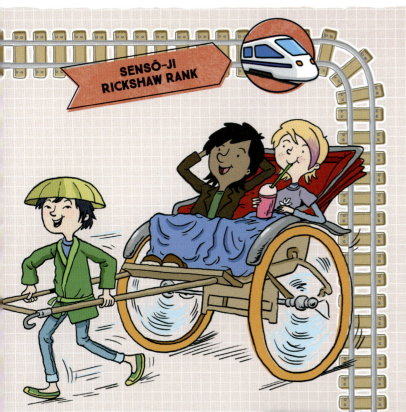

TRIP BACK IN TIME

TODEN ARAKAWA LINE

Tokyo is famous for being busy, gleaming, and modern, but there's one journey that gives its passengers a quieter, more old-fashioned experience. The Toden Arakawa Line is all that remains of a tram network that once spread across the city and dates back to 1913. The trams trundle through the north of Tokyo, past old wooden buildings, local playgrounds, tiny corner shops, and people's backyards. It's a unique way to view Tokyo — and all for less than the price of a plate of noodles in the city center.

HUMAN-POWERED

SENSŌ-JI RICKSHAW RANK

It's not all high-tech — many people walk and cycle around Tokyo under their own steam. If that sounds a bit tiring, you can always hop onto a rickshaw and pay for someone else to do the work. A rickshaw has space for two passengers (with a cozy blanket on top) and handles so that its driver can pull it along. To catch one, head to the famous Sensō-Ji temple in Asakusa — it has a row of ready-to-ride rickshaws outside.

search: RICKSHAW

📍 **MADE IN JAPAN**

Rickshaws are popular all over Asia, and can now be seen in many other cities around the world, too — but they were invented in Japan in the year 1869.

📍 **THE CLUE'S IN THE NAME**

The English word "rickshaw" is based on its Japanese name, *jinrikisha*. It simply means "human-powered vehicle."

THE LINE IS NICKNAMED "CHIN-CHIN DENSHA" AFTER THE "DING-DING" SOUND OF THE TRAMS' BELLS.

TODEN ARAKAWA LINE

LOOKING BACK

People began living in the Tokyo area thousands of years ago. Since then, it has experienced wars, battles, and revolutions, as well as periods of great art, culture, inventions, and power. The city loves to remember and celebrate its past, by way of museums, memorials, and reenactments.

THE KOFUN PERIOD (AD 250–538) IS THE FIRST RECORDED ERA IN JAPANESE HISTORY. BUT THESE PEOPLE DIDN'T WRITE MUCH DOWN, SO THERE ARE FEW HISTORICAL RECORDS. HOWEVER, THEY DID LEAVE US TOMBS, ARMOR, WEAPONS, JEWELRY, BELLS, SCISSORS, AND COOKING POTS.

START

TOKYO NATIONAL MUSEUM

SHITAMACHI MUSEUM

PACKED WITH THE PAST

TOKYO NATIONAL MUSEUM

The Tokyo National Museum in Ueno Park is packed with artifacts that reveal how people in Japan used to live, work, play... and fight each other to the death! Like many other cultures, ancient clans in Japan often buried all kinds of treasures and useful items with their VIPs when they died. The museum displays impressive suits of armor such as this one belonging to a 19th-century Edo-era soldier.

HOW WE USED TO LIVE

SHITAMACHI MUSEUM

Shitamachi means "low city." It refers to the area of Tokyo that's mostly flat, or low, around the Sumida River. Traditionally, this was where Tokyo's working population lived – people like shopkeepers, craftworkers, blacksmiths, sailors, and fishermen – while richer citizens lived in the more hilly areas to the west, called Yamanote. The Shitamachi Museum re-creates homes and living conditions from around 100 to 150 years ago, so you can experience what life was like then.

UPSTAIRS AT THE SHITAMACHI MUSEUM THERE'S A COLLECTION OF CHILDREN'S TOYS FROM THE PAST, WHICH VISITORS ARE ALLOWED TO PLAY WITH.

EDO-TOKYO MUSEUM

EDO WEEK
UENO PARK

In 2016, the first ever Edo Week festival was held in Tokyo's Ueno Park. People were invited to come dressed in Edo-style kimonos to experience what it was like in the Edo era. They could take part in craft workshops and tea ceremonies, listen to traditional music and *rakugo* (comedy storytelling), and try food – all from the Edo period.

UENO PARK IS A GREAT PLACE TO STEP BACK IN TIME. YOU'LL FIND PLENTY OF MUSEUMS, OLD TEMPLES, STATUES, AND OTHER HISTORIC ATTRACTIONS.

EVERYTHING EDO
EDO-TOKYO MUSEUM

Tokyo has only been called Tokyo since the year 1868. Before that, it was called Edo, which means "estuary." In Tokyo, people look back on the Edo period, from 1603 to 1868, as a time of great art and culture. The Edo-Tokyo Museum tells the story of how Edo grew from a fishing village, to a warlord's stronghold, to a major city, which finally became Japan's capital. It includes models of Edo people, towns, houses, and objects.

UENO PARK

"Ooh, I'd love a cup of tea."

WARRIOR KNIGHTS

THE SAMURAI

From the 1100s to the 1800s – which is a very long time – Japan was ruled by army leaders called shoguns. Samurai were high-ranking warriors or knights, who were loyal to their shogun, or clan leader, and fought on his behalf. Like the medieval knights of Europe, the samurai are famous for their loyalty, code of honor, and fighting skills.

THERE WERE SAMURAI FIGHTERS UNTIL THE LATE 1800S, AND SOME CAN BE SEEN IN EARLY PHOTOS.

SAMURAI PRACTICED THE TRADITIONAL ART OF *CHADO*, OR THE TEA CEREMONY, TO DEVELOP FOCUS, CALMNESS, AND APPRECIATION OF WHAT WAS AROUND THEM.

EN GARDE!

Even more famous than samurai armor are the razor-sharp, steel samurai battle swords. The best known is the *katana*, a long, curved sword with a handle designed to be held in both hands. Making a sword was a sacred ritual, and took a group of craftsmen several days, or even weeks, to complete. Sword lovers can admire ancient *katana* and other samurai swords at the Japanese Sword Museum in Shinjuku.

SUITS YOU!

The samurai wore amazing suits of armor, made of leather, iron, and wood, lined and decorated with silk, gold, and lacquer (or paint). As well as providing protection, samurai armor was often a major fashion statement. The Samurai Museum in Shinjuku has a huge range of armor. You can even try on a suit, practice your sword-wielding skills, and have your photo taken.

THE SAMURAI

KATANA
SWORD

search: SAMURAI SKILLS

SOPHISTICATED SOLDIERS

Despite being handy with a sword, a samurai wasn't just a lean, mean, fighting machine. As an upper-class member of society, he was expected to be highly cultured, and accomplished in a range of skills.

ROCK GARDENING

Creating the perfect rock garden (or zen garden) was a way for samurai to develop self-discipline.

CALLIGRAPHY

Calligraphy is the art of beautiful handwriting. Many great calligraphers were also samurai.

SHARPSHOOTERS

Samurai didn't just use swords – they had other weapons, too, including bows and arrows. One of their most important skills was archery on horseback. Samurai Nasu no Yoichi is still famous today for his archery feat of 1184. He shot an arrow through a fan hanging from a ship's mast, while riding a horse in the sea. In 1187, Minamoto Yoritomo, the first shogun, invented *yabusame*, which was a horseback target-shooting contest to give samurai more archery practice. *Yabusame* tournaments are still held in Tokyo, with contestants dressing in historical costume.

JAPAN AT WAR

NATIONAL SHOWA MEMORIAL MUSEUM

In World War II (1939–1945), Japan was on the same side as Germany and Italy – fighting against the Allies. Japan's part in the war began when it attacked the US naval base at Pearl Harbor, Hawaii. It ended after the US attacked Japan with nuclear bombs. This museum is all about what life was like for ordinary people in Tokyo during and after the war. You can see their letters, photos, clothes, furniture, everyday items, and gadgets.

LOYAL TO THE LAST

NOGI SHRINE

The era of shoguns and samurai ended in 1868, and Japan was once again ruled by an emperor, Emperor Meiji. But there were quite a few wars and rebellions, including the Satsuma Rebellion in 1877. It had nothing to do with fruit, but was an uprising of samurai who were annoyed that they no longer had a big role to play. Maresuke Nogi was an army general who fought on the emperor's side. He was so devoted to his master, he offered to kill himself when things went wrong. The emperor refused his offer, so instead, Nogi and his wife killed themselves when the emperor died in 1912. There's a shrine to honor their loyalty in Akasaka, near the home where they died.

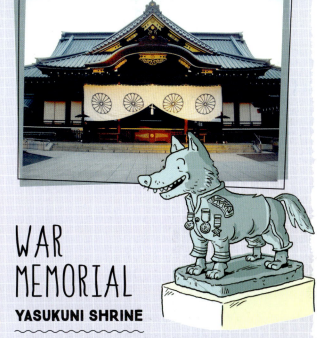

THE HORROR OF WAR

CENTER OF THE TOKYO RAIDS AND WAR DAMAGE

In the months before the nuclear attacks in August 1945, the US firebombed Tokyo. Over 100,000 people died. This museum may have a clunky name, but it aims to help people understand the value of life by showing what happened to Tokyo's citizens in 1945.

FIREBOMBS (WHICH START FIRES) WERE USED ON TOKYO BECAUSE IT HAD MANY TRADITIONAL BUILDINGS MADE OF WOOD AND PAPER, WHICH WOULD BURN EASILY. PAPER WASN'T USED FOR THE MAIN WALLS, BUT FOR LIGHTWEIGHT SLIDING WALLS USED TO DIVIDE ROOMS.

WAR MEMORIAL

YASUKUNI SHRINE

This shrine near Chiyoda Park remembers those who have died in war fighting for Japan. Inside, the names of about 2.5 million of them are listed. They include not just humans, but also animals that have been involved in wars, such as dogs and horses. There are animal statues outside the shrine, too.

AFTER WORLD WAR II, JAPAN FOCUSED ON REBUILDING ITS CITIES AND INDUSTRY AND BECOMING A MODERNIZED NATION. IN JUST A FEW DECADES, IT BECAME A WORLD LEADER, ESPECIALLY IN TECHNOLOGICAL INDUSTRIES. THE COUNTRY'S TRANSFORMATION IS KNOWN AS AN ECONOMIC MIRACLE.

YASUKUNI SHRINE

FUN AND GAMES

Like plenty of other nations, the people of Japan love playing and watching sports and games. Some of these are well known and popular around the world, while others are uniquely Japanese...

START

RYŌGOKU SUMO STADIUM

ARASHIO-BEYA SUMO STABLE

JUDO
SIMILAR TO WRESTLING, THIS MARTIAL ART WAS INVENTED IN 1882.

AIKIDO
IN THIS FORM OF SELF-DEFENSE, YOU USE YOUR OPPONENT'S STRENGTH TO DEFEAT THEM.

KARATE
THIS MARTIAL ART USES PUNCHING, KICKING, AND "KNIFE-HAND" (CHOPPING) TECHNIQUES.

KENDO
KENDO IS SIMILAR TO FENCING, USING SPECIAL ARMOR AND BAMBOO SWORDS.

SPECTACULAR SUMO

RYŌGOKU SUMO STADIUM

This is the place to go in Tokyo to watch top-level sumo wrestling. It's a huge, purpose-built stadium that can hold up to 10,000 spectators. In the middle is the ring, or *dohyō*, with a temple-like roof suspended over it, so that it seems to be floating in midair. Bouts of sumo don't take very long. To win, one wrestler must push the other over or out of the ring, which often happens in a few seconds. The crowds also come to see the ritual exercises and parades in between the matches. After an especially exciting match, or if a top wrestler is defeated, everyone throws their seat cushions into the ring.

SEE INSIDE A STABLE

ARASHIO-BEYA SUMO STABLE

Sumo wrestlers don't live normal lives – they have to live, eat, sleep, and train in a special sumo stable, or *beya*. Some *beya*, such as Arashio-Beya, let tourists watch the morning training session, or *keiko*. But visitors must treat the *beya* with great respect – no snacking, chatting, or waving selfie sticks is allowed!

Sumo has existed for over **1,000 YEARS**, and started off as a Shintō religious ritual.

For fighting, wrestlers wear just a **MAWASHI**, which is like a thick belt combined with underwear.

There are **NO FEMALE** professional **SUMO WRESTLERS** – in fact, women are not allowed into the ring at all.

MARTIAL ARTS AND MUSIC STARS

NIPPON BUDOKAN

Japan is famous for martial arts such as judo and karate, which combine fighting skills with mental focus. The Budokan is Tokyo's arena for the country's many martial arts championships. Its bowl-like shape also means it makes for a cool concert hall, and it's famous for hosting music stars such as the Beatles, Bob Dylan, and Mariah Carey.

NIPPON BUDOKAN

TOKYO DOME

TOKYO DOME IS NICKNAMED THE "BIG EGG"!

STRICT RULES MEAN THE WRESTLERS MUST WEAR TRADITIONAL CLOTHES AND HAVE LONG HAIR IN A *CHONMAGE*, OR TOPKNOT.

BASEBALL BANANAS!

TOKYO DOME

In the late 1800s, Japanese society began to be strongly influenced by the US. One of the biggest imports of all was the sport of baseball. The Japanese LOVE baseball and see it as their national sport. Schools, businesses, towns, and cities all have teams, and tournaments are must-see TV. As well as being used for festivals and concerts, Tokyo Dome is the home of the famous Yomiuri Giants. It also has a baseball museum inside, recording the rise of the sport in Japan.

NIHON KIIN

LET'S GO!
NIHON KIIN

Go, also called *Igo*, is an old board game – really old! It was invented in China about 4,000 years ago, and spread all over Asia. The game has two players who use black and white stones to try to surround areas of the board, or *goban*. The rules are simple, but it takes lots of practice and concentration to play well. In the 1600s, Japan actually had a minister of *Go*, who set up *Go* schools and contests, and people still play it today. The Nihon Kiin in Ichigaya, the headquarters of Japan's *Go* Institute, has a *Go* "salon" where people can play, and a shop selling *Go* gear.

MEIJI-JINGU GAIEN PARK

search: **1964 OLYMPIC GAMES**

📍 **JUDO ASIA FIRST**
The Tokyo Olympics in 1964 were the first Olympics ever held in Asia.

📍 **WAR IN THE WAY**
Japan was meant to host the Olympics in 1940, but the games were cancelled because of World War II.

📍 **REMEMBERING HIROSHIMA**
Sakai Yoshinori, the torchbearer who lit the cauldron at the 1964 games, was a student and amateur sprinter, and was born on the day the nuclear bomb fell on Hiroshima in 1945.

ACCORDING TO AN ANCIENT PROVERB, *GO* TAKES "A FEW MOMENTS TO LEARN, A LIFETIME TO MASTER."

OLYMPIC PARK
MEIJI-JINGU GAIEN PARK

This park in Shinjuku is sports heaven. It has tennis, baseball, and futsal (mini-soccer) courts, a rugby stadium, an ice rink, and a golf range. But there's more – this was the home of the Japan National Stadium, where Tokyo hosted the Olympic Games in 1964. In 2015, the old stadium was torn down, to be replaced by a new one for the 2020 Olympics.

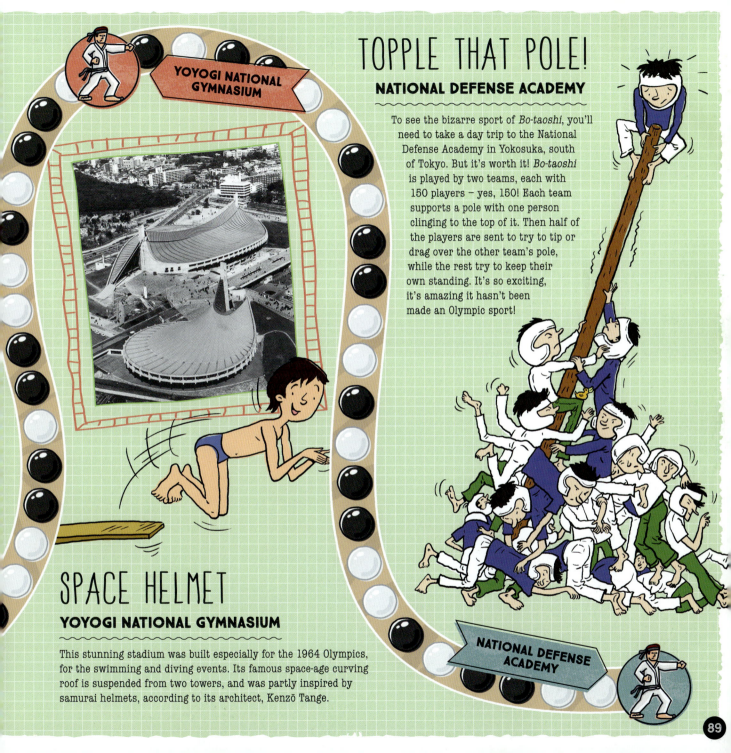

YOYOGI NATIONAL GYMNASIUM

TOPPLE THAT POLE!

NATIONAL DEFENSE ACADEMY

To see the bizarre sport of *Bo-taoshi*, you'll need to take a day trip to the National Defense Academy in Yokosuka, south of Tokyo. But it's worth it! *Bo-taoshi* is played by two teams, each with 150 players – yes, 150! Each team supports a pole with one person clinging to the top of it. Then half of the players are sent to try to tip or drag over the other team's pole, while the rest try to keep their own standing. It's so exciting, it's amazing it hasn't been made an Olympic sport!

SPACE HELMET

YOYOGI NATIONAL GYMNASIUM

This stunning stadium was built especially for the 1964 Olympics, for the swimming and diving events. Its famous space-age curving roof is suspended from two towers, and was partly inspired by samurai helmets, according to its architect, Kenzō Tange.

NATIONAL DEFENSE ACADEMY

CHRYSANTHEMUM THRONE

Japan has a long line of emperors and empresses dating back so far that the first ones are lost in legend. In fact, it has the longest-running royal family in the world. The monarch hasn't always actually ruled the country, but for over 2,000 years, there's always been someone on the throne – the Chrysanthemum Throne, as it's known.

ROYAL RESIDENCE

THE IMPERIAL PALACE

In the middle of Tokyo is a huge green area, surrounded by moats and filled with flowering trees. Inside stands the Imperial Palace, home of the Japanese royal family. It was built on the site of the old Edo Castle, the headquarters of the shogun, or military ruler, in the Edo period. During World War II, it was mostly destroyed, and then it was rebuilt. Despite all that, some of the walls and towers of the old castle are still standing.

YOU CAN COME IN!

Twice a year, once on January 2 (for New Year) and once on the emperor's birthday, the public is allowed to cross Nijubashi Bridge and go inside the palace. There, people can see the royal family, who stand on a glass-covered balcony. The emperor makes a speech, then everyone waves flags.

IMPERIAL PALACE

ACROSS THE MOAT

Japan's most famous bridge, Nijubashi (meaning "double bridge"), leads over the moat and into the private palace area. There are actually two bridges, one made of stone and one of iron. Much like the palace itself, they're not very old, as they've been rebuilt several times. The bridge is also nicknamed *Meganebashi*, or "spectacles bridge." Why? Because when the two arches of the bridge are reflected in the water, it looks like a pair of glasses!

search: IMPERIAL FACTS

📍 **660 BC**
This is the date the monarchy is said to have begun, making it more than 2,500 years old.

📍 **EMPEROR JIMMU**
The legendary Jimmu is remembered as Japan's first emperor. So far, there's no proof he existed, but there are many stories about him.

📍 **NICE NEIGHBORHOOD**
House and land prices close to the Imperial Palace are among the highest in the world.

SWAN STORY

BEAUTIFUL SWANS GLIDE TO AND FRO IN THE PALACE'S TRANQUIL MOAT, AND ARE FED AND CARED FOR BY PALACE STAFF. ACCORDING TO LEGEND, EMPEROR SUININ, WHO IS SAID TO HAVE REIGNED AROUND 2,000 YEARS AGO, HAD A SON WHO COULD NOT SPEAK. BUT HE STARTED TALKING AFTER HEARING THE CALL OF A FLYING SWAN. IT'S SAID THE ROYAL FAMILY HAS PROTECTED THEM EVER SINCE.

HERE'S YOUR ROOM!

AKASAKA PALACE

If you're a visiting VIP or head of state, you'll get to stay here – Akasaka Palace, the State Guest House. With its marble pillars and fabulous fountain, it's considerably grander than the buildings of the Imperial Palace. Famous guests include Ronald Reagan, Margaret Thatcher, and Barack Obama – but when it's less busy, there are days when it's open to the public.

> THE PALACE LOOKS UNLIKE ANYTHING ELSE IN TOKYO. IT WAS BUILT AROUND 1900, WHEN JAPAN WAS STRONGLY INFLUENCED BY WESTERN STYLES, AND MODELED ON FANCY STATE BUILDINGS IN PLACES LIKE PARIS AND LONDON.

MEIJI THE GREAT

MEIJI SHRINE

Emperor Meiji was the first emperor to return to power after the end of shogun rule, in 1868. He was only 15 at the time! He went on to oversee the modernization of Japan. The Meiji Jingu, or Meiji Shrine, surrounded by a forest in central Tokyo, honors Emperor Meiji and his wife, Empress Shoken. Nearby is a garden of irises, which the emperor created for Shoken, as they were her favorite flower.

MEIJI SHRINE

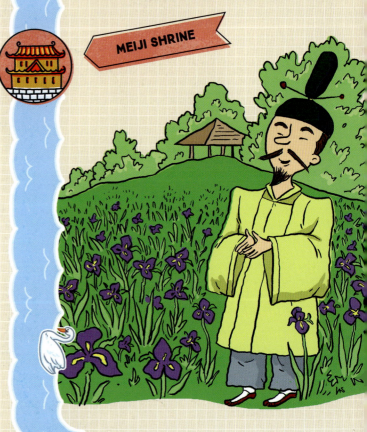

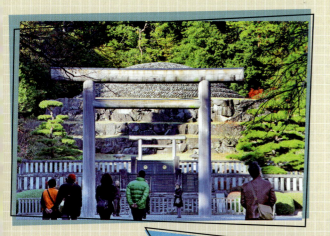

SAGAMI BAY

SEEKING SEA CREATURES

SAGAMI BAY

Emperor Hirohito was Japan's monarch for much of the 20th century, including during World War II. Although being emperor was a demanding job, he was also obsessed with marine biology – the study of sea creatures. The royal family had a vacation home to the south of Tokyo at Sagami Bay, where Hirohito would search for interesting sea life specimens. He even had a special laboratory built at the Imperial Palace, where he sorted and studied his finds.

WHEN HE DIED, IT WAS REPORTED THAT HIROHITO WAS BURIED WITH HIS MICROSCOPE AND HIS MICKEY MOUSE WATCH, AS HE WAS A BIG FAN OF DISNEY ANIMATIONS.

MUSAHI IMPERIAL GRAVEYARD

REST IN PEACE

MUSAHI IMPERIAL GRAVEYARD

Far from the hustle and bustle of central Tokyo, in a quiet park in the suburbs, lie two great emperors, Meiji's son, Emperor Yoshihito, and his son, Emperor Hirohito, alongside their wives. After death, Japanese emperors have their names changed – so they are now known as Emperor Taisho and Emperor Showa.

RECENTLY, ALL OF JAPAN'S MONARCHS HAVE BEEN MEN, AND BEING EMPRESS HAS MEANT BEING THE EMPEROR'S WIFE. BUT IN ANCIENT TIMES, THERE WERE EIGHT RULING EMPRESSES. THE FIRST, EMPRESS SUIKO, REIGNED FOR 35 YEARS IN THE LATE 500S AND EARLY 600S.

"I'm exhausted. Feel like a drink?"

MAXXI

TODAY'S ROME

MAXXI

This striking contemporary building was designed by star architect Zaha Hadid. It houses Rome's premier contemporary art museum. It doesn't look Ancient Roman, but perhaps the ancients might have appreciated its geometric shapes, metal columns, and steps. The Renaissance and Baroque designers would probably have covered it with all sorts of elaborate decoration!

THE FIRST MALL

TRAJAN'S MARKETS

The Ancient Romans built high-rise buildings, with shops on the ground floor and houses and offices behind and above. This big three-story semicircle was one of the world's first shopping malls with added offices and apartments – a 2,000-year-old version of what we see in modern towns. Now it's just another ancient ruin.

TRAJAN'S MARKETS

search: **ANCIENT ARCHITECTURE**

📍 Ancient Roman architects developed things like:

amphitheaters – to provide the space for popular entertainment, like audience-participation TV shows today

aqueducts – to move water (like modern plumbing)

domes – to amaze; they are still used in cathedrals, mosques, palaces, and to cover indoor rainforests!

MODERN DREAMWORLD
RAINBOW MAGICLAND

In Rome's theme park, 20 minutes outside the city, anything goes. It is full of enchanted-looking buildings entirely based on the magical world of the imagination. There's a fairy school, a wizard's madhouse, a ghost ship, and even a mysterious castle that hides a super-speedy roller coaster.

QUARTIERE COPPEDÈ

FANTASY FUN
QUARTIERE COPPEDÈ

This small Rome neighborhood has its own fairytale architecture. There are buildings with turrets, swirly sculptures, Arabic arches, and scary gargoyles. This fantasy style is called Art Nouveau and was popular when the buildings were designed in 1919 by the architect Gino Coppedè.

RAINBOW MAGICLAND

HEAVENLY HANAMI

WELCOMING THE CHERRY BLOSSOM

Tokyo has many thousands of trees, and the most beloved of all are the cherry trees, or *sakura*. Every spring, when cherry blossoms bloom around late March or early April, people celebrate the arrival of spring with *hanami*, or "flower-viewing."

PACK YOUR PICNIC!

The traditional way to do *hanami* is to have a picnic or party underneath a blossoming cherry tree in the spring sunshine with your friends or family. Or you can have your picnic in the evening – in many areas, the blooming trees are lit up at night with pink lanterns. Don't forget to bring *sakuramochi*, a sweet pink rice cake wrapped in cherry leaves.

WHAT DOES IT ALL MEAN?

Besides looking nice and heralding spring, the cherry blossom has a symbolic meaning in Japan. Its beauty lasts for only a short time, acting as reminder that life is short and precious, and nothing lasts forever. It is linked to the Japanese concept of *mono no aware*, a combination of joy and melancholy about the things around us.

HANAMI
(FLOWER-VIEWING)

search: CHERRY BLOSSOM

BLOOMING EVERYWHERE
No one knows exactly where the first ever cherry tree grew, but now it grows all around the world.

ANCIENT TRADITION
People in Japan have celebrated the cherry blossom season for at least 1,000 years.

WATCH THE WEATHER
As cherry blossom time approaches, Japan's weather forecasters keep track of when the blossoms are blooming further south, so they can predict when they will open.

TOP SPOTS

There are several favorite areas around the city for enjoying the frothy pink blossoms at their best. They include Ueno Park, Shinjuku Gyoen National Garden, and viewing the trees from a cruise on the Sumida River. The Imperial Palace gardens are also full of cherry trees, and the moats end up covered in the fallen blossoms.

CHERRY BLOSSOM CULTURE

BECAUSE CHERRY BLOSSOM IS SO IMPORTANT IN JAPAN, YOU CAN FIND IT IN ALL KINDS OF ARTISTIC CREATIONS. IT'S MENTIONED IN TRADITIONAL SHORT POEMS CALLED *HAIKU*. IT APPEARS IN MANY OLD PAINTINGS, AND IT IS ALSO USED IN MODERN DESIGNS. THERE'S ALSO A FOLK SONG ABOUT IT, "SAKURA SAKURA."

VIA DEL GOVERNO VECCHIO

PALAZZO DE CUPIS

DON'T WAVE BACK!
PALAZZO DE CUPIS

On moonlit nights, a ghostly hand is said to appear at a window of the Palazzo de Cupis. It once belonged to a lady called Costanza Conti de Cupis, who lived here in the 1600s. Her hand was so beautiful that an artist made a model of it, but one day a stranger saw the model and predicted that Costanza would soon lose her hand. Terrified, she hid indoors to stay away from harm, but one day she pricked her finger while sewing. Her arm became badly infected and she eventually had to have her hand cut off, though it didn't save her. She died but her hand is said to haunt her home.

BUMPS IN THE NIGHT
57 VIA DEL GOVERNO VECCHIO

Something weird went wild in this house in 1861, according to reports from the time. There were loud thuds, and objects were thrown through the air and smashed against walls. Eventually, the terrified owners left, though not before a number of eyewitnesses, including police officers, confirmed the mysterous goings-on. It sounds like the work of poltergeists, the messiest ghosts going. *Aiuto!* (Help!)

search: ANCIENT ROMAN GHOSTS

FICTIONAL PHANTOM

The world's first-known ghost story was written by Ancient Roman author Pliny the Younger. It tells of a man who buys a house at a bargain price, only to find a noisy, chain-rattling ghost popping up to bother him inside. Later a chained skeleton is found buried in the courtyard and after giving it a proper burial, the haunted homeowner finds peace at last.

CARRIAGE FULL OF COINS

PONTE SISTO

The ghost of Olimpia Maidalchini, the sister-in-law of Pope Innocent X, is said to ride across this bridge in a black carriage, carrying crates of gold coins and laughing like a witch. In life, she was the pope's adviser in the 1600s and was hated by locals, who nicknamed her the *Pimpaccia* (wicked woman) because they thought she made herself very rich at everybody's expense. When her protector, the pope, lay dying, she knew she was in danger from her enemies, so she escaped Rome in her black carriage, taking the pope's treasure boxes with her. She died of the plague two years later.

PONTE SISTO

PIAZZA VITTORIO EMANUELE

DARE YOU KNOCK?

PIAZZA VITTORIO EMANUELE

A mysterious, spooky-looking door flanked by two strange figures is all that remains of a villa where the Marquis Palombara lived in the 1600s. The story goes that the marquis once met an alchemist who told him he knew how to turn ordinary metal into gold. The next day, the alchemist had disappeared but he had left behind some gold flakes and gold-making instructions, written in symbols that nobody could read. The marquis had the instructions carved on his doors in the hope that a passer-by would understand them and knock, but nobody ever did. The weird symbols above the door still mystify visitors.

INDEX

A Bathing Ape (shop) 43
Akasaka Palace 92
Akihabara 30, 75
amusement arcade 66
animal cafés 94
animals 71, 94–7, 98, 99
anime and manga 16, 26, 27, 33, 54–7
Aokigahara Forest 12
Aoyama 43, 47
Aoyama Technical College 24
aquariums 9, 19
Arasho-Beya Sumo Stable 86
architecture 22–5
  see also skyscrapers
art 16, 52, 56, 58–63
Asahi Beer Headquarters 23
Asakusa 37, 60, 63, 75
Audi Forum 25

baseball 87
bathrooms 34, 49
bell-ringing 70
black eggs 14
boating 48, 67, 77
bonsai 29
Botaoshi 89
bullet trains 76

cable car rides 13
capsule hotels 29
Center of the Tokyo Raids and War
  Damage 85
Character Street 57
cherry blossom 96–7
Cup Noodle Museum 38

Daikanransha Ferris Wheel 19, 20

Earthquake Hall 10
earthquakes 10–11
Edo-Tokyo Museum 81
entertainment and nightlife .. 64–7, 72–5

fashion and style 42–7
Ferris wheel 19, 20
festivals 19, 21, 40, 68, 81
fireworks 19
fish 6–9
food 6, 7, 8–9, 14, 36–41, 55
fugu (pufferfish) 9
Fujifilm Square 34
Fujiwara, Hiroshi 42

game centers 16, 35
Ghibli Museum 54
Ginza 68
Go Institute 88
Godzilla 15, 73
'golden poop' (Asahi Beer Hall) 23
golf 66
Gotoku-ji 94

Hachiko statue 95
Hachioji 48
Hakone 14
Haneda Airport 21
Harajuku 41, 44–5
harbor tours 67
haunted Tokyo 12, 48–53
helicopter tours 20
Hibiya Park 69
Himiko water taxi 77
Hokusai, Katsushika 60–1
Hokusai Museum 61

hot springs 14–15, 65
Iidabashi Subway Station 22
Imperial Palace 90–1, 97
Inokashira Park 48
Institute for Nature Study 99
Intermediatheque 99
islands 15, 59
Izu Oshima 15

J-pop 75
Japanese Sword Museum 82

Kabuki theater 74
Kanda Myojin Shrine 31
Kanto Earthquake Memorial Museum .. 10
Kappa-Dera Temple 53
Kappabashi Street 40
Karaoke Kan 64
kawaii 26–9, 33
Kawaii Monster Café 27
Kiinokuni Slope 51
kimonos 46, 81
kite festivals 21
koi carp 8
Koishikawa Korakuen Gardens 8
Kusama, Yayoi 59
Kyary Pamyu Pamyu 45

Leisureland 66
'light architecture' 18–19, 66, 67
Lotte Kasai Golf 66

markets 6, 67
martial arts 86, 87
Maruhan Pachinko Parlour 71

Masakado Shrine 51
Meguro Parasitological Museum 95
Meiji Shrine 92
Meiji-Jingu Gaien Park 88
Mode Gakuen Cocoon Tower 17, 19
Moomin House 28
Mori Tower 16
Mount Fuji 11, 12–13, 17
Mount Mihara 15
movies 54, 65, 73
murals 56, 58, 59
Musahi Imperial Graveyard 93
Museum of Contemporary Art 62
museums 10, 15, 29, 30,
   31, 32, 34, 35, 36, 38, 53, 54, 58, 61,
   62, 78, 80–1, 82, 84–5, 95, 99
music, traditional 75

Nakagin Capsule Tower 23
National Art Center 58
National Defence Academy 89
National Museum of Nature
   and Science 30, 32
National Showa Memorial Museum 84
National Theatre of Japan 73
Ni-Tele Really Big Clock 55
Nihonbashi 76
Nijubashi 91
Nippon Budokan 87
Nippori Fabric District 47
Nogi Shrine 84
Noh theater 53, 72
noodles 38–9

observation decks 11, 16, 17, 18, 21
Odaiba Takoyaki Museum 36
Oiwa-Inari Tamiya Shrine 50

Oiwake 75
Olympic Games 88
Omiya Bonsai Art Museum 29
Omoide Yokocho 41
Omotesando 42
onsen (spas) 14, 65
Origami Kaikan 98
Ota Market 67
Owakudani 14

pancakes 8, 36, 41
parks and gardens 8, 33, 48, 67,
   69, 72, 81, 97
PauPau Aqua Garden 6
photography 34, 55
pinball 71
Pokémon Center 57
police boxes 23
Pompompurin Café 26
puppet theater 73
Purikura-No-Mecca 55

Rainbow Bridge 66, 77
Reversible Destiny Lofts 25
rice crackers 37
rickshaws 79
Risupia, Odaiba 35
Robot Park 33
robot technology 32–3
Roppongi Hills 16
royal family 90–3
Ryogoku Sumo Stadium 86
Ryogoku Sumo Town 37

Sagami Bay 93
St. Mary's Cathedral 22
samurai 45, 51, 82–3, 84

Samurai Museum 82
SanrioWorld Ginza 27
Sea Paradise Aquarium 9
Seaside Park 67
Senso-Ji Temple 68, 79
Shakaden Reiyukai Temple 24
Shibuya 109 43
Shibuya Crossing 69
Shimo-Kitazawa 46
Shin-Bungeiza 65
Shinjuku 64
Shinjuku Gracery Hotel 73
Shinjuku Gyoen National Garden 97
Shinjuku Station 52, 70
Shirohige's Cream Puff Factory 55
Shitamachi Museum 80
Shonen Theme Park 56
shopping 6, 26, 27, 28, 30, 40, 42–3,
   46–7, 57, 64, 67, 68, 69
shrines 31, 50, 51, 84, 85, 92
skyscrapers 11, 16–19, 49
Skytree Town 19
Sony Explorascience 35
Sou-Sou, Aoyama 47
spas 14, 15, 65
sports and games 86–9
street sculpture 16, 52, 59, 62
subway system 22, 70, 76, 78
Suginami Animation Museum 54
Sukeroku tiny toys shop 28
sumo wrestling 37, 86–7
Sunshine 60 49
sushi 7

taiyaki 8
Takadanobaba Station 56
Takarazuka Revue 74

INDEX

Spanish Steps 87

sports 76–9

Square Colosseum 90

Stadio Olimpico 76

starling migration 61

statues 22–3, 24–7, 58, 59, 63, 67, 77, 81

Swiss Guard 67, 70

"talking statues" 22

Tarpeian Rock 39

Teatrino di Pulcinella Gianicolo 49

Tempietto di Bramante 91

temples 7, 8, 9, 92

tennis 76

Terme di Caracalla 17

Testaccio 14, 89

theater 49, 50, 51

Theater of Marcellus 50

theme park 95

Tiber Island 17

Tower of the Monkey 30

toy shops 88

Trajan's Column 23

Trajan's Markets 94

Trevi Fountain 20–1, 53

Turtle Fountain 18

Vatican City 57, 63, 65–7, 75, 79

Vatican Museums 32–3, 38, 67

Vespas 73

Vestal Virgins 9

Via dei Condotti 69

Via del Corso 30, 87

Via della Gatta 59

Via Margutta 86

Via Sacra 6

views of Rome 28–9

Villa Borghese 80–1

Villa Celimontana 85

Villa del Priorato di Malta 28

Villa Doria Pamphili 83

Villa Giulia Museum 81

Villa Torlonia 82

Vittoriano, il 24, 29

Vittorio Emanuele II 24–5

walls, city 52

Walls, Museum of the 52

Zoo 61, 80

FURTHER READING

Horrible Histories: Rotten Romans
by Terry Deary and Martin Brown

Go back in time to visit the ancient Romans in all their grungy glory. This book celebrates all that is most fun and foul in this historic city.

Eyewitness Ancient Rome
Dorling Kindersley

This book is perfect for school projects on Ancient Rome – it's full of information about emperors and gods as well as everyday Romans.

The Cities Book
Lonely Planet Kids

This worldwide travel guide aimed at kids is crammed with really useful information on lots of cities, including Rome.

Michelangelo for Kids: His Life and Ideas, with 21 Activities
by Simonetta Carr

Find out all about the artistic genius and the Renaissance, then learn some of his techniques. Maybe you could create your own masterpieces after completing all the activities in this book!

The Thieves of Ostia
by Caroline Lawrence

This children's novel brings Ancient Rome alive as it follows a young dectective and her group of friends all around Rome uncovering secrets and solving mysteries.

The Orchard Book of Roman Myths
by Geraldine MacCaughrean and Emma Chichester Clark

Packed full of Ancient Roman myths that describe how Rome was created and who the Roman gods and goddesses were in a simple way that all children will love.